PHANSITE.COM

ThE LAst AmErIcAn Gypsy
was initially published as part of
WElcOmE tO ThE LAnd Of CAnnIbAlIstIc HOrsEs
(Puberty Press, 2005)

All writing Copyright 2005 A.P. Smith
All photography copyright 2005 A.P. Smith
All art copyright 2005 Mike Force

A BRIEF INTRODUCTION FOR THE 2016 EDITION

Twelve Years Later, Twelve Years Older

In 2004, Phish announced they were breaking up. And for so many of us, it was devastating news. They had previously taken a hiatus for two years, but this time it was for good. In Trey's letter detailing the break up, he wrote: "For the sake of clarity, I should say that this is not like the hiatus, which was our last attempt to revitalize ourselves. We're done."

Of course, they've since reunited.

And so, the title of this book, The Last American Gypsy, now seems wrong or inaccurate. Phish got back together and, resultantly, the American Gypsy lives on! Considering the massive scale of recent Phish shows (Riviera Maya, MagnaBall), not to mention the cosmic magnitude of the Fare Thee Well shows, one could argue that the American Gypsy is more alive, more prevalent now than in the timeframe of this book.

For a current 22-year-old, right now may very well be the height of his or her freedom and connection to the music. It certainly was for me. In 2004, I had just celebrated my 22nd birthday, had just graduated college, and had spent that Summer following my favorite band across the USA... Can you imagine? The freedom!

Looking back on it now, that's what this book is really about: travel, adventure, and freedom, specifically the freedom of youth and its vast highway stretched out before you with no end in sight as you rocket down the road.

Then suddenly, it's all over. Time is up.

Phish was over and we had to say goodbye, goodbye to the band, goodbye to our friends, our jobs, our home on the road… Phish offered all of that and more to a lot of people, and going into the final festival knowing this was the end cast a dark shadow across the whole experience. Calling it bittersweet is an understatement. We were all just trying to make the most of it, what we had left. Unfortunately, that weekend at Coventry every hello was also a goodbye. Looking back on it now, Coventry seems like a long weekend of hospice after a terminal Summer tour.

For me personally, Phish disbanding may have forced my hand in life. With Phish, we could travel and live in the moment, show to show, with little cares or concerns beyond getting to the next show. But without Phish, where would we go? Without Phish, what would we do? Without Phish, we had no choice but to move on, to move on to what would quickly become adulthood.

Now, I'm 34 years old. I'm engaged to be married, own a small terrier dog, and for the last four years I've held down a traditional 9am-5pm marketing job. And while my responsibilities are not as grand as some of my friends with children or mortgages, I'm far from the splendor and spontaneity of my 22-year-old Phish tour days.

Though my fiancée would scoff at that. She'd be quick to remind us that this Summer I travelled to Minnesota to see Phish. And then saw Phish for two nights at Wrigley Field in Chicago. And after that, I took the train to Philly and caught two nights there. Then I joined some friends in Saratoga for three more shows before meeting her at the show in Mansfield. And then Hartford too.

What's more is that in two days we're flying to Denver for three more Phish shows.

So I suppose it's fair to say that even with matrimony on the horizon, my Phish days are far from over. And what may be considered "adulthood" has not yet kept me from Phish tour. This Summer I saw 10 shows. And my fiancée, after I introduced her to the band, has now seen Phish nearly 20 times, I think 17 shows last we counted?

But it's different now, people say. Hell, I've said it too. And what we mean is that it's not as good. Though some of the Summer 2015 shows, particularly Philadelphia and the final night in Colorado, were some of the best performances I've ever seen, which is important to note: 12 years after their breakup and 7 years after their reunion, Phish is playing at the peak or near peak levels of their musicianship.

This book was initially published in 2005 and Phish reunited in 2009. Since then, they've released two new studio albums and played 309 shows, including a momentous three-night New Years run at Madison Square Garden in 2013 to celebrate the band's 30th anniversary, four epic Halloween shows, three massive weekend festivals, and their live premiere south of the border in Mexico.

And so what's to come? Tales of Adulthood on Phish Tour? The *Next* American Gypsy? That sounds more like a reality show than anything else. But hey, these days you can live stream the show on your laptop, follow setlist developments in real time on Twitter, and even download mp3s of the show for free using a code on your ticketstub.

Has Phish jumped the shark? If I can still find adventure and freedom at Phish shows, then surely no. At least not yet.

I've never counted how many shows I've seen. Probably 100 shows? Maybe more. I suppose it would've made sense to count after Coventry, after they said goodbye when that number would've been finite and unchanging. Now it feels too late? Or irrelevant?

And maybe the same can be said about this book.

Maybe revisiting this chronicle of Phish's final / not-final tour is a moot point now that they've since gotten back together?

Or maybe this book isn't really about that. Maybe it's not about the band at all. Maybe it's not about my experiences on the road, doing drugs, dancing barefoot. Maybe it's not about coming of age and saying goodbye and growing up and finding adulthood.

I don't know. Maybe so, maybe not.

Ask me at the next show. Or better yet, ask my fiancée?

- A.P. Smith
8/30/16

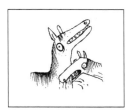

I'm pulling the pavement from under my nails
I brush past a garden, dependent on whales
The sloping companion I cast down the ash
Yanked on my tunic and dangled my stash

Zipping through the forest with the curdling fleas
To grow with them spindles, the mutant I seize
I capture the dread beast who falls to his knees
And cries to his cohorts, asleep in the trees

Smegma, dogmatagram, fishmarket stew
Police in the corner, gunnin' for you
Appletoast, bedheated, furblanket rat
Laugh when they shoot you, say
"Please don't do that"

Control for smilers can't be bought
The solar garlic starts to rot
Was it for this my life I sought?
Maybe so maybe not

Maybe so maybe not...

-Tom Marshall and Trey Anastasio,
Phish lyrics

I boarded the plane and sat next to a tall man cramped in his seat in row nineteen. I said hello, immediately pulling out my notebook not only to write out the events of the last few days, but also to avoid a potentially inescapable chat with a Southern Stranger.

"Where you headed?" he asked.

"Home to New York," I said.

We proceeded to chitchat fittingly until I noticed he was wearing the same purple T-shirt as most of the overweight, middle-aged passangers, in fact, the exact same T-shirt as every single man sitting around me.

"Are you an athlete?" I asked.

"No," he laughed. "We're missionaries. Our leader organizes these trips to Romania every year to build buildings and feed food to the gypsies. This is only my third year but some of them have been nine and ten times and our leader has been all over the world."

His T-shirt breast pocket insignia was a map of the world, eastern and western hemispheres, split by a Christian cross.

"Yeah, it's something, you know," he continued. "We go over there and build houses and churches, even though we're non-denominational, we have Christians and Baptists and Church of God, and well, it's just that these gypsies have endured generations and generations of racism and persecution so that they stick to their own. The Romanians don't even understand why we come to help them. They say, 'why are you helping the dogs?' A lot of people think we have it pretty bad over here, but I think we just take a lot for granted."

"I think you're right," I said. "That's amazing what you're doing."

The Southern Stranger nodded proudly yet modestly, like a good God-fearing Christian. "What were you in Virginia for?" he asked. "Family?"

"No, I had a court date."

"Traffic ticket?"

"No," I said. "I was arrested for selling beer at a Phish concert."

"Phish, huh?" he asked. "Did you go to their last concert up where it was?"

"Vermont? Yeah. That was a great time. Bittersweet, but I have no problem with them calling it quits."

"They picked up after The Grateful Dead, right? Kind of followed what they were doing?"

"In a sense, I guess. There are a lot of similarities between the scenes. The Dead were certainly first but I don't really think of Phish as Grateful Dead Junior."

The Southern Stranger laughed and pretended not to notice that he elbowed my arm off the armrest. "So you'd just follow them around from show to show?"

"Sometimes," I said.

"How many shows have you seen?"

"Around fifty."

"But it's a different show every night?"

"Yeah. Yeah, it is."

And he nodded, and I nodded, and then nothing. We were both silent. The chitchat was over if I wanted it to be.

I thought for a moment.

"Tell me more about the gypsies."

THE LAST AMERICAN GYPSY
CHRONICLES OF PHISH TOUR 2004

PART ONE

Thieving WaWas & Waffle House Rendezvous:
On Trial Near Naval Base Norfolk

There was no ATM at the Days Inn. The one at the Red Roof Inn was out of money, and the ATM at Hooters was out of order. My buddy Brian and I were tired of walking and wanted to head to the lot, so he gave me the ticket and I told him I'd give him the sixty as soon as I sold some beers. Brian, a sharp-nosed, business-type Wall Street intern, is a nice guy like that, always willing to help out a friend. On our way we stopped by his hotel room where I took a shit and we sat to smoke a joint.

"Sylvia couldn't make the show?" I asked. Sylvia is his girlfriend, a sweet girl whom I met once in Miami.

"She's sick, not doing so well," Brian said, separating the blue pills from the yellow pills in his hand. He picked out two and tossed them in his mouth; I did the same. "She's got leukemia, probably only a few months left."

The pills went down hard. "I'm sorry," I said.

Brian nodded, spilling out another bottle of pills onto the wobbly hotel room table. "Want some morphine?"

"Sure," I said, eating more pills, and watching Brian pour some cocaine onto the table and roll up a twenty-dollar bill. After a few rails we left to meet up with the rest of his people standing near his car in the hotel parking lot drinking beer from red plastic cups. I recognized all of them from shows past but only remembered Bubba's name. He looked like a Bubba: stocky, fat even, with enormous hands and beady little eyes. Everyone was happy to see each other and we drank a few beers before walking towards the lot, towards The Mothership.

The Mothership, or Hampton Coliseum, is a fantastic place to see a concert. On the outside it looks like a giant crown, concrete and stoic in its symmetry during the day, and extraterrestrial at night. Different colored lights illuminate the hollow recesses of each equilateral spire, and the coliseum seems mere seconds from lift off. It brings to mind space travel and especially so for those of us who believe aliens built the pyramids. I also believe aliens built Hampton Coliseum. All seating is general admission and there isn't a bad seat in the house.

The first time I went to Hampton Coliseum was with Sam for the New Year's run 2002. On New Year's Eve in New York we didn't score a ticket for the Madison Square Garden show but we didn't give it much effort. Instead we simply people watched and drank tequila and when the tequila was gone we left the Garden and took the train to a house party in Williamsburg where we danced and drank champagne until five in the morning. Three hours later we were in a cab to JFK.

At the terminal curb I couldn't even smoke a cigarette, I was so hung over, still drunk really. The tequila/champagne crossover is an ugly one best avoided. I was prepared to shit or puke at any moment.

And then we boarded our airplane: a sparrow puddle jumper with seats for twenty-two passengers. Sam and I had seats 1A and 1B, facing Victor, our smooth-faced African American flight-attendant whose seat bottom folded out from the wall opposite our seats. During take-off, my kneecaps rattled against Victor's kneecaps but he kept his eyes closed.

Sam and I stunk of booze. Our bodies were on the verge of violent purging and collapse. God damn right Victor kept his eyes shut. Eventually, Victor stood up, resumed his attendant duties, and the airplane took on a high-pitched hum and vibrated at such a cadence that if you focused your eyes on the window pane the glass went fuzzy. I felt drunk all over again and my own stench made me salivate, what we all know as a foreshadowing and often a point of no return type of mouth-watering before vomiting.

The whole flight was rough and as we pulled down to land, only about fifty feet and closing from touchdown, Sam lurched forward and yanked the air-sickness bag from her seatpocket next to Victor and puked only what sounded like a mouthful but smelled like disease and sour milk, dead flowers, and it was everything I could do to keep myself from following her lead.

One time I watched my friend Sparky in Seattle puke on a public telephone so I puked on it too. We were already drunk when we hit the bars and after a few $2 pitchers of Red Dog, some hash we bought, smoked, and lost on the street, and an altercation with a gas station clerk, we came across a payphone near the university campus. This was just after payphones made that ten cent leap from twenty-five to thirty-five and Sparky, just like you and me, made a nemesis out of each and every payphone he saw and the payphone that night was no exception. In our stupor we hammered rocks at the silver change box to take back what we've spent since the increase, but we didn't even scratch it. Then we found bigger stones and threw them at the machine but that made only small dents in its armor. Finally, Sparky announced that we should just fucking puke on the thing and hurled a night's worth of alcohol, stomach bile, and what looked like meatloaf all over the payphone. "Your turn!" he yelled, not bothering to wipe his chin.

But on the airplane I didn't puke, a good thing because as soon as Sam folded the top of her soggy airsick bag she reached for mine and puked again as we taxied on the runway. Victor, the professional that he was, announced the temperature and time without missing a beat, all the while handing Sam wetwipes and napkins. I gave him a little slap on the thigh to show I was impressed and he smiled nervously. "Once again, I hope you arrive safely to your final destination," he said over the intercom. "And if you've reached it here, welcome to Norfolk."

We took a cab from the airport to the hotel I booked near the Naval Base. Percy Widget, our cab driver, yes, that was his name, white rat-tail and large rings on his fingers, was once in the Navy, had never been to

New York, and just loves to drive.

Norfolk, like Fayetteville in North Carolina, is a town comprised of and sustained by the military. Like most military towns, a poor neighborhood with little development surrounds the base. Our hotel was situated in the most desolate part of that neighborhood next to a box-shaped building with no markings, only a neon Budweiser sign in the window. We said our thankyous to Percy and entered the lobby, which looked just like a living room: area rug, paintings, empty cofee cups. An Indian couple sat in matching recliners facing the afternoon soaps on television. Little dialogue was exchanged; our room was ready, we checked in, paid cash.

Once in the room I fell onto the bed and my eyes shut closed. Even in that long-anticipated surrender of willpower against exhaustion, I could tell Sam had not moved from the doorway.

Okay, I'll admit it, the room was below par. The sheets were dirty and pockmarked with cigarette burns, brown smears on the walls, the toilet water was yellow, and the room smelled overwhelmingly like an open field on a summer day. I spent a few minutes trying to persuade Sam to stay—it's just three nights, we've paid, all that—nothing worked.

We took a cab to another hotel in downtown Norfolk and stayed on her parents' dime. At three in the morning, when she was sleeping and I was watching a movie, an air raid siren sounded and I didn't know what to make of it or the strobe light flashing on the wall. It was a fire alarm of the most ghastly sort. Sam stayed in bed, but downstairs myself and one other middle-aged Phish fan stood sleepless in the lobby. We exchanged nods. I think he made some joke, and we talked about how far we'd come and what time we arrived. When the alarm stopped he said he'd see me tomorrow and we rode different elevators to our rooms.

The next day around noon Sam and I hitched a ride from the hotel to the coliseum and our entrance was smooth and unimpeded unlike when I returned three years later.

I jumped ship a few hundred yards from the Waffle House and walking along the freeway, past parked cars and trucks and vans weighed down by patient and anxious half-drunk twenty-somethings listening to classic rock music and Phish concert bootlegs, I smiled at a half-dozen roadside loiterers with raised index fingers hoping someone would sell them a ticket.

Miracle seekers.

I would have joined them if Brian hadn't promised me his extra ticket.

Besides, I had no cash after the incident at the Wawa gas station so when I found Brian, after we hugged and smiled at each other, we went looking for an ATM.

Earlier, at the Wawa gas station/convenience store, after eating breakfast at a different Waffle House, I decided to stock up on beer and cigarettes to fund this last run of concerts. After Hampton we planned to drive to Mansfield, Massachusetts for two shows, then skip Camden and drive straight to Coventry, Vermont for the Phish's final concert, a two day festival and I needed to buy enough to sell enough to get me through to the end. I shopped wisely. The beer would have to be bottles, some variety, a nice domestic and a something cheaper. I chose Yuengling and Budweiser and carried case after case to the counter where I requested a few cartons of Camel Lights, Marlboro Lights, and Marlboro Reds, in all $300. I had just over $100 cash, and so I withdrew $200 from the ATM. But when I was paying, I realized the ATM only gave me ten ten-dollar bills and looking at my receipt, yes, the machine charged my account for the full $200.

    The gas station of the South is not that much different from the gas stations of the North or the West or even Middle America. When driving day and night, every day and night, fluorescent lighting can come to be a source of comfort or nourishment. The gas station is a sanctuary, a provider. And when that ATM ripped me off at the WaWa in Virginia, I felt scorned, betrayed, as if my own mother had thrown me out on the street.

    "Your ATM robbed me!" I told the clerk.

    "Sorry," he said. But he didn't really mean it. "You can talk to the manager."

    I argued fiercely with the Wawa manager but no money was recovered or reimbursed and after causing a general fuss that worried some of the customers, I finally gave up. I borrowed a hundred dollars from Kelly, paid the $300, stole six bags of ice, and we boarded Tim's GMC Yukon to drive the last twenty miles to The Mothership.

    I didn't have a ticket for the concert. I didn't have any cash. I owed Kelly $100. I owed Tim $45 for gas. I had no pot. But I what I did have would resolve each of those dilemmas. $300 worth of cold beer and cheap cigarettes would yield me profit to the degree of which I would make, subtracting my own consumption, enough money to come out of tour with the same amount I had going into it. But that's hardly ever the case.

In Miami for the 2003 New Year's Run, Sam's little brother, Jeff, and I sold beer we bought at Costco in bulk and made $400 profit the first night and almost $200 the second night and would have done better but that second night there was a lot of nitrous around and I got caught in the pitfall of trading beers for balloons. The third night, after the concert, Jeff and I made almost $300 in twenty minutes.

The dynamic of supply and demand in Phish lot is interesting because there's never a shortage of either. For every person selling beer, there is someone buying beer, and thousands of them. I've been on both sides of the scale and I'll tell you something: if you plan on driving 2,000 miles, seeing a dozen concerts, paying for gas, food, and lodging, you better have something to sell along the way. Bartering works too, especially amongst veteran fans, but selling beer and cigarettes—the only two legal substances almost anyone will buy even if it means spending their last five dollars—is the most lucrative business on Phish tour.

When Brian, his friends, and I reached the lot I split from them to find Tim and get my beer. At six feet, ten inches, with long burnt red hair and matching goatee, Tim isn't hard to spot in a crowd. I found him talking with an old friend with whom we had planned to share a hotel room at Camden last year. We didn't find him that night in Camden, or he made himself scarce, and we ended up sleeping in the car because there was no room at the inn. I wasn't interesting in catching up with that asshole so Tim gave me the keys and told me where he had parked. Soon, I dug out Cara's skateboard to rest the hundred pound cooler on top to roll the beer to Shakedown Street, the main drag of the parking lot, where all the vendors and pushes loiter.

You tell me this town ain't got no heart. well, you can never tell.
The sunny side of the street is dark. well, well, well, you can never tell.
Maybe that's 'cause it's midnight, in the dark of the moon besides.
Maybe the dark is from your eyes, maybe the dark is from your eyes...
Nothin' shakin' on shakedown street. used to be the heart of town.
Don't tell me this town ain't got no heart. you just gotta poke around.

You think you've seen this town clear through.
Well, well, well, you can never tell.

THE LAST AMERICAN GYPSY

Nothin' here that could int'rest you. well, well, well, you can never tell.
It's not because you missed out on the thing that we had to start.
Maybe you had too much too fast. maybe you had too much too fast...

-Lyrics to Shakedown Street. (The Grateful Dead)

Shakedown Street comes in many shapes and forms but is nothing more and nothing less than a market place, a meeting ground, the main drag, community square, a walkway where T-shirts, alcohol, drugs, artwork, paperbacks, concert tickets, glass-blown pipes, and food exchange hands. Anything you need or want on Phish tour can be bought or traded for on Shakedown. The economy of Phish tour, especially for those of us going from show to show, is primarily isolated and self-sufficient. If you were to follow the path of a dollar spent on Shakedown, chances are it would still be circulating on Shakedown four concerts later, across three state lines. Excluding the initial capital for a pusher to buy a pound of marijuana or a vendor to buy the ingredients for 200 chicken gyros, all the money on Shakedown stays on Shakedown, unless, of course, you spend it on $8 beers inside the venue or your intentions are solely to make back the money you spent on tickets through either mail-order or God-forbid Ticketmaster.

Standing next to my opened cooler at the tail of Shakedown in a less populated, less vendor-regimented area, I drank. In no time at all, people were buying my beer. As soon as I put the cash in my pocket someone else wanted a beer. For a moment someone selling Magic Hat beer stationed himself nearby and stole all my customers but business picked right back up again. Occasionally I sold a pack of cigarettes. And when Brian and Bubba found me I had more than enough to pay Brian for the ticket and I gave them both a beer.

"Doing well?" Brian asked me.

"Well enough," I said.

"Can I have another, Andy?" Bubba asked me. He had already slammed his beer.

"How much?" some long-haired hippie boy asked me. He was holding his wallet and the crowd of people milling behind him had doubled. The lot was filling up.

"One for three, two for five," I said, pulling out two beers. He gave me a five, took his beers, and walked away.

"How're you feeling?" Brian asked me with a crooked smile.

"Not bad, not bad," I said. The coke had worn off but the uppers were working and in combination with the blues and the morphine, I was feeling somewhere between super-quick and a-okay.

"Can I get two?" someone asked me.

"Sure," I said and we traded beer for cash.

"Here," Brian said, holding out his closed hand. "I'm gonna take another beer."

I pocketed the pills he handed me and asked if I could buy some coke. He shook his head no and instead dug out a thumbnail-sized blue baggie and handed it to me. "Just take it." It looked like half a gram.

"Thanks," I said slipping the baggie between the cellophane and the box of my cigarette pack.

"Can I get a beer?" someone asked Brian.

"Yeah," he said, handing him a beer for three singles. Then he handed the money to me.

Brian and I chatted about the drive down and made guesses as to what song Phish would open with and Bubba disagreed with everything we said. I opened a beer for myself and lit a cigarette and suddenly a rush of patrons blitzed my cooler and I couldn't sell them beer fast enough. Brian and Bubba helped and when the mob subsided, they gave me my money.

"Thanks for helping guys," I said. "But in the future, just direct them to me. It's just too many hands, too many exchanges, just point them to me next time."

Then someone else wanted a beer and after the transaction I turned to Brian who just sold four beers to some middle-aged man wearing a neon pink strip club T-shirt and an American flag baseball cap. The man handed Brian a ten and stood still for a moment before turning and walking aimlessly. When Brian tried to hand me the ten, I refused to accept it. "You just sold to a cop, man! I'm not touching that money."

"What are you talking about, it's fine."

"No," I said. "It's not fine." I looked around for the arriving smackdown but saw no one in the crowd who looked out of place. Looking back at Brian, I watched two plainclothes police officers show him their badges and then a third officer showed his badge to me. All three cops wore T-shirts and jeans and had five days growth on their face. Through the crowd I could see the American flag hat next to a uniformed police officer.

THE LAST AMERICAN GYPSY

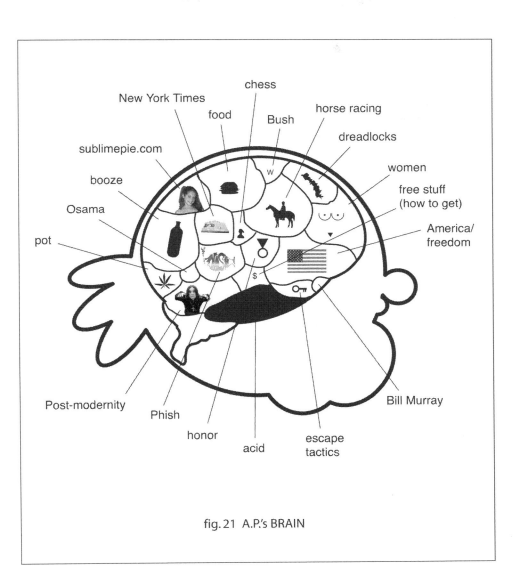

fig. 21 A.P.'s BRAIN

"If you coorporate, you can still go to the concert," the officer told me. "Now grab one end of the cooler and come with us."

"No problem, officer," I said.

Cops are like lovers: if you put in just a little effort and consideration, it'll come back to you ten fold. Most of the time.

Brian was a little more aggravated than me and verbally resisted the officers who obviously wanted to make this as clean and unnoticeable as possible.

"Just come with us," the cop said.

"Brian, let's handle this, okay?" I said, remembering the pot, blow, pills, and cash I had in my pocket.

"You have ID, son?"

"Sure, officer," I said and handed him both my military ID and my driver's license.

"Grab the other end," the officer ordered.

I grabbed one end of the cooler and tucked Cara's skateboard under my arm and walked with the plainclothes cop behind Brian and the other two arresting officers. As we walked away from Shakedown and through the lot only a few of the Phish fans we passed were aware of what was happening. Of those observant concert-goers, some glared and snarled at the police but many more looked at me empathetically but relieved, relieved that for at least this one short moment they were out of harm's way.

"Washington state, huh?" the cop asked me. He put on his sunglasses. We were walking farther and farther away from Shakedown. "You're a long way from home."

"Actually, I live in New York now, just finished college and thought I'd catch one more concert before I started my new job," I said, proud of my pandering.

"Where'd you go to school?"

"Pratt Institute in Brooklyn."

"What kind of school is that?"

"It's an art school," I explained, happy to keep the chitchat going, hoping that I looked sober, more importantly that I sounded sober. The uppers were losing against the morphine and I was beginning to think my speech was slurred. "I studied writing."

"What kind of writing?"

"All kinds. Mostly travel writing."

"You're not gonna be writing about this are you?"

"You bet I am, officer," I said.

That comment ended our chitchat.

We walked in silence, sharing the weight of the cooler. My grip was weakening. "How much farther?"

"Not far now."

I saw the destination: a black van parked by itself in the farthest corner of the parking lot where other plainclothes cops waited for our arrival. The reunion of this law enforcement team was one of celebration, a mission successful; these men had returned with the hippies they sought out.

"Why don't you just have a seat here on the cooler, Andrew," said my officer. "Just sit tight." And he left to join the rest of them with Brian on the other side of the van. When I was massaging the aggression out of my cop, who knows what foul language Brian spat and now I reaped my reward, alone on the cooler, they searched and interrogated Brian behind the van and out of sight. I looked over my shoulder but saw nothing. I contemplated eating the pills or tossing them and the blow but decided instead to relax, take a deep breath, and open a beer from the cooler.

While I sat drinking a woman walked by and offered me ecstasy, rather Molly, a slang term for pure MDMA, the active ingredient in ecstasy.

"No thank you," I said, smiling. She trotted off and I finished my beer. I glanced again over my shoulder and made eye-contact with one of the arresting officers who stared at me until I turned away. Twenty minutes passed and long after that, as soon as they finished with Brian, my cooler-pal cop approached me with a form he had filled out and squatted down next to me to ask for my signature.

"I can't sign that," I said.

"It's not an admission of guilt," the cop explained, rubbing his face, the stubble that obviously itched him. "It's just to say that you know you have a court date to appear for."

"Why do I have a court date?"

"For selling alcohol without a liquor license."

"But I wasn't selling alcohol."

"Listen son," the cop said, scooting closer and removing his shades. "You have to sign this. If you don't sign this I have to arrest you and you will spend the night in jail."

I read it over and signed.

"And now, our officer says you were selling cigarettes too."

I remained silent.

"Can I look in your sack?"

He was referring to the plastic bag I had full of cigarette packs. I handed it to him.

"Where'd you buy these?"

"Wawa."

"In Virginia?"

"Yes, sir."

I watched the cop inspect each pack checking for state seals, and he was satisfied to find them.

"I tell you what," he said, putting his sunglasses back on. "I'm gonna let you keep your cash, usually we take everything you have." He waited for me to thank him and when I didn't he continued. "And I'm gonna let you keep your cigarettes, but I have to take your cooler."

"I can't let you take the cooler," I said. "It's not my cooler, I'm borrowing it."

And what he said next, he spoke in that tone that allows you to hear what the speaker really means. It's like when you're talking to someone and you're not really listening so you just keep saying "uh-huh," what you're really saying is "shut the fuck up." What this cop said, in that special tone, caught the attention of the other cops and they gathered around us. Then he said it again: "Excuse me?"

But what he really meant was "What the fuck did you just say to me?"

"Officer, I'm sorry," I said. "Take the beer, but I can't let you have the cooler."

The three cops stood with their hands on their belts and looked at each other. Neither one wanted to speak first.

"I don't have a problem with that, do you?" one said, scratching his ear.

"I don't have a problem with that," said the other, rubbing his eye.

"Okay, open it up," said the last, rubbing his mouth.

I had ten beers left. Yuengling, but less than a case, and the cops started removing the bottles and placing them in a box with what looked like two cases of other miscellaneous beer bottles. When there were only five or six bottles remaining in the cooler I asked the police if they would be kind enough to leave me just a few for myself and my friend.

"I don't have a problem with that, do you?" one said.

"I don't have a problem with that," said the other.

Brian came around the side of the van and stood nearby. He was silent, perhaps scared or beaten into submission. The poor bastard looked broken. It was time to leave, and leave with what we still had.

I closed up the cooler and plopped it on the skateboard and was ready to push off when the asshole American flag cap cop approached me, saying, "Hey! Hey!"

"Yes?"

He got right up in my face and with sour breath and a pointed finger against my chest he said, "You owe me ten dollars."

I almost bit his fucking nose off. But no, I used restraint and simply gave him ten dollars, not *the* ten dollars that Brian still held, but ten dollars toll to make my escape.

Walking away, Brian cursed and blasphemed all the way back to Tim's car. They had searched him, found everything, confiscated everything, even the sixty dollars I paid him for the ticket. He was pissed and I had no desire to reprimand him again for selling my beer to a police officer.

The morphine was really on top of me.

Throughout centuries of gypsy persecution, non-gypsies have created laws aimed at keeping gypsies on the move or at least away from town. Gypsies the world over have been targeted as criminals, if only because they're gypsies. This lawful segregation and oppression and alienation doesn't in fact deter the gypsies; it only pushes them to the fringes of contemporary society. These laws do not impose conformity but rather frustration and anger on both sides.

I hit Shakedown to warn a few friends I knew were selling beer.

"I know," a buddy said. "It's like I'm selling drugs!"

One friend I warned promptly removed her court summons from her back pocket, displayed it proudly, and we hugged.

"I'll be damned if I'm gonna show up tomorrow!" she said.

"Your court date is tomorrow?"

"Isn't yours?"

I checked my summons.

"Those bastards know none of us are going to be in town tomorrow!" she yelped. "Goddamn them!"

"Those bastards," I mumbled.

"Need any Molly?" my friend asked.

Suddenly I was jumped on from behind and heard screaming in my ear. It was my friend Selene and she was with Cara.

"Thanks so much for getting my girl down here!" Selene said.

"Anytime," I said.

"Didn't I tell you he was amazing?"

Cara smiled, slightly embarrassed.

Cara and I had just met and she seemed interesting, a lively Long Islander, definitely burnt out. She looked like she may have been cute at one time but drugs and tour had sucked all that out of her. Or maybe not all of it. She was a friend of Selene, who I knew from college, and when Selene called me to ask if I was making it to Hampton she asked if I could find a ride for Cara. The day before the concert I called Cara and asked her to meet me at Union Square where Tim would pick us up.

Tim was already forty minutes late and Cara and I had run out of topics to discuss. The New York City street crowd stomped past us with

occasional looks of curiousity or contempt.

"You don't have a cup do you?" Cara asked.

"No, why?"

"We should be begging for change right now," she said. "Everyone's looking at us like we're homeless."

I was sitting on my giant pack with my sleeping bag rolled up at the bottom and Cara had her skateboard, a purse, and a purple plastic bin full of 150 already-made veggie burritos.

"A sign maybe," I said. "You don't have a marker do you?"

"No."

"Me neither."

More people walked past frowning, not missing a beat in their steps or conversations.

The next day on Shakedown in Virginia Cara, Selene, and I smoked a joint and drank some of my friend's beer and bitched about the cops and then I took Cara back to Tim's car so she could stash something. What it was she didn't tell me and I didn't ask. That would have been rude.

At the car, locking up, a dirty, strung-out tour rat approached us.

"Hi, Cara, you look well," he said.

"Hi, James. You look like shit."

"You're always so pleasant, Cara," he said, with knees bent as if he expected to faint at any second. His sweatshirt, stained and torn, thinning, looked like it was the only top he owned. "Where are you sitting tonight?"

"I'm not sure yet," she said, ushering me along, walking us away.

"It's always a pleasure to see you," he called to us.

"Clean yourself up, James," Cara replied, linking arms with me as we walked. "That's my ex-husband," she said. "Looks like he's still on the horse."

I didn't say anything. The pills and the booze were working nicely. I was glad to have linked arms with her. Glad she had an ex-husband. Glad she was talking as we walked through the parking lot, down aisles and between cars, cars with license plates from New Jersey, Illinois, Georgia, Florida, Pennsylvania, and very few from Virginia.

The Hampton show was to be my forty-somethingth, maybe forty-fifth or forty-sixth Phish show and while to some of you reading this that may seem like an excessive amount, I know that some of you have seen two or three times that. By no means do I claim to be an expert or an aficionado. I know only what I know about Phish tour and wish to tell a tale of my experiences and observations of that subculture, that community. Above all, know this: I go to Phish concerts, like most people, for the music and all else is lagniappe. Each show is different, and that spontaneity, the connection that occurs between audience and musicians after a series of concerts, the familial community, all of that lengthened my time on tour and today informs my recollections of those years.

And the show that night at The Mothership could have been better. Phish played lazily that night. Sure the audience was tired from the drive, but we were also excited to start this last run, one final tour. Everyone I talked to the next day said the concert disappointed them. Even six weeks later at my rescheduled court date, my newfound courtroom pew-mate said, "That show really just wasn't worth it."

That kid, that poor kid, he was facing a possession charge and when he stood before the judge the arresting officer read his report and it was apparent that the kid was fucked. They found a baggie in the glove compartment of his car because he was smoking a joint when they pulled him over. Fucked. He stood there quivering and in his defense he read from a folded photocopy of Virginia legislature. He claimed innocence on article 17.8 C: marijuana is constituted by vegetative growth and not the seeds or steams of the plant. Basically... I smoked it all... and so there was none left... so... I'm innocent...

Someone in the courtroom coughed "bullshit."

Mama Judge looked up at the courtroom then at the kid and slammed the gavel. "Guilty," she said and suspended his license and fined him $155.

I twitched in the pew. Something just didn't seem right. I'm facing a $500 fine if found guilty for selling beer and this tadpole possesses marijuana, was caught using marijuana, and gets off paying just $155?

The side door of the courtroom opened and I watched two fat, black bailiffs—one looked just like the cop in the *Die Hard* movies—escort into the courtroom a lanky, shaggy haired twenty-something wearing an orange jumpsuit and leg shackles. He had deep-set eyes and walked comfortable in the bailiffs' arms, like he had been doing it for weeks, probably six weeks, the six weeks since the concert. I made eye contact with him as the bailiffs sat him down. He leered at me, then mouthed the words, *I... need... a... cigarette.* Then he flashed me the peace sign.

A woman from the second pew stood up and met with a man who was obviously the kid's attorney. They asked Mama Judge for a moment to discuss the charges.

The judge left the room and the hippie's attorney talked with the prosecutor while the hippie and the bailiffs talked about *Chappelle's Show*. I eavesdropped on both conversations catching what I could. The attorneys were planning a compromise involving some loophole in the legislature that would allow him to go free today despite being arrested at the Phish concert with three pounds of pot and two pounds of mushrooms. The bailiff, the one from *Die Hard*, was telling the hippie all about the last episode of *Chappelle* and how much he liked it when Chappelle made fun of white people. Then the judge returned and we all stood up.

In the end, everyone was pleased. The hippie got eleven years suspended sentence with six weeks time served and was escorted out of the courtroom to be discharged and released.

"Now hearing the case of Mark Simmons," the prosecutor announced.

My turn would come soon. And I was ready. I didn't spend $300 on airfare and a hotel room to be found guilty. I could have easily been tried in my absence and simply paid the fine like most friends who faced the same charge. No, I wanted them to see my face and my long beard and my dreadlocks and realize I had done nothing wrong and ask me to have mercy on the court and forgive the officers present. I was prepared to go against the state of Virginia and lose, but at least I would lose honorably.

Although, the whole trip had been filled with fortunate outcomes. I had planned to stay up all night to make my 6:35 am flight but passed out on cheap wine just before sunup and jolted awake at 6:05. I called a cab, grabbed my phone, and headed outside where the cab was already waiting for me. "Hi, how are you I'm very late please go as fast as you can to JFK," I told the driver.

"Fine, thank you," he replied, and the cab lurched forward continuing to gain speed.

I made my flight. I've never missed a flight. But when I deplaned in Norfolk I realized that I had neither my court summons, still tacked to my bulletin board in Brooklyn, nor any money to my name. I was broke and my most recent check had yet to clear. Fortunately, a kind sailor knew exactly what court house I needed to go to, and a generous Baptist woman in a bright red business suit and hat offered to share her cab because she was going that way anyway. So the fact that I made it to the courthouse at all demonstrated that the Gods were looking favorable upon me.

I had talked to Brian earlier in the week and he said he had asked for a continuance and his date was rescheduled. I figured that would work in my favor.

Waiting in the hallway outside the courtroom a few of us Phish fans killed time talking about the band while all the arresting officers sat quietly and patiently. When a flat-faced man in a suit approached me and asked me what my name was I asked him what his name was. Turns out, he was a police officer and after looking at my file he said my specific arresting officer, Officer Bowers, was on leave due to a death in the family and my court date would need to be rescheduled.

"No, I'm here," I said. "I'm here, let's take care of it."

"You can talk to the prosecutor, but I'm sure he'll tell you the same thing," he said. "He's that man over there."

"Well, remind me of your case again," the prosecutor said. He was a thin man with no sign of malice or self-righteousness. His brow was smooth and unblemished.

"I was arrested because a friend of mine sold my beer to an undercover cop," I told him. "I didn't sell the beer, but got in trouble when I admitted the beer was mine. I live in New York and I flew down here to take care of this today."

"Okay," he said, switching his briefcase from hand to hand. "I'll just throw the case out."

So I was feeling good in the courtroom watching the state of Virginia crucify the ill-fated Mark Simmons.

PROSECUTOR: Officer Jackson were you working on the afternoon of August ninth?
OFFICER: Yes, I was.
PROSECUTOR: And were you indeed working Coliseum Boulevard during the Phish concert that afternoon?
OFFICER: Yes, I was.
PROSECUTOR: And did you observe the individual present sell liquor without a liquor license?
OFFICER: Yes, I did.
PROSECUTOR: What did you observe?
OFFICER: Well, at 3:57 pm I observed the subject, later revealed to be Marc Simmons, drinking a twelve ounce bottle of Budweiser beer near the main walkway to the coliseum and because of his youthfulness I remained in a position where I could observe his actions. After observing him sell two twelve ounce bottles of Budweiser to another subject, I approached Mr. Simmons and requested to purchase a beer. He then sold me two twelve ounce bottles of Budweiser beer for five dollars at which time I revealed myself, confiscated the beer, and issued the summons.
JUDGE: How do you plead?
SIMMONS: Guilty.
JUDGE: And what do you recommend, sir?
PROSECUTOR: Five hundred.
JUDGE: Guilty as charged. Five hundred dollar fine.

Mark Simmons left the courtroom and the prosecutor called my name. I walked to the judge and stood next to the prosecutor. The judge's hair glistened in the light and her glasses cast a glare over her eyes.

"I see here that Officer Bowers is on leave," the judge said, reading my file. "This hearing is rescheduled for October twenty-seventh."

"Your honor, may I say something?" I asked.

She looked at me.

"I live in New York, I just graduated from college, I'm taking time off my new job to spend the money to fly down here and stay in a hotel for the night. I was not notified that my court date was to be rescheduled and I'd like to settle this now, while I'm here."

"You'll have to come back on October twenty-seventh," the judge said.

"I won't be able to," I said. My conviction rattled her.

"And why is that?" she asked.

"Because I've spent all the money I have to be here today."

"And how do you plan on pleading?"

"Not guilty, your honor. The beer was mine, yes, but I was not selling it."

"Son," she leaned in and pushed her glasses up to the bridge of her nose. "You're going to have to come back."

Perhaps it was a mild acid flashback or some cathode ray tube branding but suddenly I felt like Princess Leia at Jabba's palace demanding the bounty for the great wookie, Chewbacca.

I looked at the prosecutor for help, some sort of guidance.

He evaded my glare but finally spoke up: "Your honor may I have a minute with Mr. Smith?"

The judge sighed. "We'll take a short recess."

I followed the prosecutor into the hallway where he let his posture weaken and unbuttoned his blazer. "What's your problem?" he asked.

"What's my problem?"

"What's your problem with my case?"

"My problem is that I'm not guilty and I'm not coming back so let's deal with this now. My problem is that it isn't my fault the cop didn't show up. My problem is that I've already spent three hundred dollars. I guess you could say I have a few problems."

The prosecutor stared me down and I stared right back.

For a moment I thought he was going to hit me.

"How do you feel about plea bargaining?" he asked.

"I'm listening."

"What if I amended the docket to read that you weren't selling the beer but did have an open container in your possession?"

"What's the fine on that?"

"Twenty-five dollars."

"Alright, let's do it," I said, leading us back into the courtroom.

THE LAST AMERICAN GYPSY

That night I drank a twelve-pack in the hot tub at the Hampton Radisson, passed out early, woke up late, and had the cabbie stop at a gas station for a carton of smokes on our way to the airport.

About two months later I heard from Brian. He had appeared for his court date in October. And so did all four arresting officers.

They butchered him on the spot.

PART TWO

Entry Wounds, Exit Wounds:
Beautiful Landscapes Can Be Dangerous

There are only three bands I would drive hundreds of miles to see: (1) Phish, (2) Soul Coughing, (3) Morphine. Soul Coughing broke up, Phish is now broken up, and the lead singer of Morphine is dead, fucking died on stage. I feel old.

But I guess growing old is just a soft, peaceful synonym for survival.

I was sixteen years old when my mother took me to my first Phish concert. We had just moved from Fayetteville, North Carolina to Seattle, Washington and that summer I listened to live Phish bootlegs and watched almost every game of The World Cup. Then summer yielded to Autumn, I started my junior year of high school, and Phish scheduled a stop of their Autumn tour at The Gorge at George, Washington.

The geography of Washington is such that clouds come in from the coast so heavy with rain that they hang lower than the peaks of the

Cascades and, crashing against the side of the mountains, the clouds drop their rain upon Seattle and the surrounding regions. The mountain range acts as such a powerful divide that Eastern Washington receives almost no rainfall and feels like another state entirely. The drive east on I-90 is beautiful: long, straight airport runways of freeway through occasional farming towns.

Reaching closer to the Columbia River the terrain changes again, this time from desert to rock and canyons. The highway clings tightly to the edge of a chasm as you make your way further east, past the Wild Horse Monument, which, at the top of a steep hill, can be seen from a distance. A herd of rusty iron horses, each about ten feet high, maybe ten or twenty horses in all, are frozen mid-gallop following their leader to certain death off the edge of the cliff.

You enter the gates, they tear your ticket, give your pockets a pat, and send you on your way down an asphalt roadway alongside a man-made pond reflecting the last of the afternoon light, that thirty minutes between day and dusk. All the concertgoers who enter with you look radiant and peacefully anxious, some walking briskly with teethy grins, others hand in hand one step at a time up this road that steeply inclines and inclines and inclines and when you reach the summit all that is real or true or beautiful in this world is presented to you like an oil painting, so detailed and full of life that it seems almost more accurate than the landscape it depicts.

Below the ever reaching bright blue sky is a rolling thickly grassed hill that tiers into stone steps towards the bottom before the floor facing the stage that stands on the edge of a massive chasm, a canyon, a gorge at the bottom of which is a shimmering cool blue ribbon that is the Columbia River.

And that, dear reader, is a shameful illustration, albeit the best I can do. Describing The Gorge is like describing heaven. Everyone's heaven looks just a little different. And my heaven isn't your heaven. But I do know this: The Gorge, hidden among the vineyards and canyons of Eastern Washington, is undoubtedly the best music venue in this country.

And yes, I've been to The Red Rocks Amphitheater in Colorado. That's a nice venue too. Perhaps if I first saw Phish at Red Rocks, I would not have the love and loyalty that I do for The Gorge. That first concert, September 16th, 1998, was wonderful. And I've never listened to that show since then. I've had opportunities, many heads on tour have tried to give me the bootleg recording, but I would rather remember the show as I do now then attempt to revisit it. I remember that autumn sunset and how Phish stopped mid-song so the drummer, Jon Fishman, could play a drumroll as the planet rotated and the sun fell down behind the chasm walls of The Gorge.

Each summer some of my friends from high school organize a camping trip and for 2003 we arranged to stay on the Columbia River not far from The Gorge. The plan was to camp for eleven nights, the last two being the Phish concerts. Only five of us, myself included, made the initial drive to the campsite in Rob's truck, towing his father's boat, an ample sea vessel for fishing and inner-tubing.

We left Seattle at dusk and after a few hours, just over the pass, we arrived in Ellensburg, Washington, home to Central Washington University, where we met up with some girls, girls Rob knew from Central, who had an apartment where we could crash before driving the rest of the way to camp in the morning. They seemed like nice girls, the frumpy, uptight type, but nice nonetheless. It's interesting how the word nice, in certain context, has come to mean mediocre. But they did make us drinks and entertain us briefly before we hit the bars.

We were drinking at some pool hall with fluorescent lightening and I found some cute tattooed girl who was curious about the big city and general Brooklyn life. I was enjoying myself and the drinks were cheap. The bar was full of muscular men with pooka shell necklaces and gelled hair and my boys were playing pool against a pair of them. I stuck out like I usually do in such places. Central and eastern Washington rarely see a dreadlocked, bearded boy with seemingly no concern for his appearance. And this tattooed girl was happy to be seen talking with him. I don't mind being that novelty. Occasionally, it gets me laid.

One of these local boys approached me and the girl stopped talking. I looked at him and he just continued to look at me. His eyes were glazed over and he held his arms crossed against his chest.

"Can I help you?" I asked.

"What's up with all this?" He asked, motioning with his hand around my head, my dreadlocks, my beard.

"What's up with all that?" I asked, motioning around his head, his short, spiked hair, his clean-shaven face.

He laughed and then seemed to be angry with me. He started yelling drunkenly and his friends, apologizing for him, pulled him out of the bar.

"Does that happen a lot?" the girl asked me.

One hot summer night in 2000 I was drinking at a bar in Boulder, Colorado and I started talking to this man with a ragged facial scar wearing a Members Only jacket and I upset him when I told him I wasn't Rastafarian. The man was completely crazy, which is so obvious to me in hindsight, but that night I didn't realize the level of his dementia until he pulled out a knife. "So if I attack you, are you going to fight back?" he asked. "If I stab you right now you're gonna bleed, and you're gonna die, don't you pacifists get that!" He waved the blade around in the air and made a short jab at me. "What's wrong with you fucks? I'm stronger than all of you!"

I slowly, calmly stepped backwards, moving away from the man, never turning my back on him. I think I told him I needed another beer, that I'd be right back.

In Ellensburg that night, the tattooed girl made off with some farm boy and my friends and I went back to the girls' apartment. My friend Steve and I hung around outside smoking a joint and talking about his ex-girlfriend, this beautiful redhead who said she may or may not show up during the campout. "Yeah, fuck her," Steve said, taking a drag off the joint, the last drag. He stomped it out with his Etnies.

I don't really see Steve any more. Occasionally when I'm in Seattle I run into him on the street or at a party, but we rarely talk. For years Steve and I were close friends. We used to drive his Bronco to various parking spots, make-out points, in west Seattle overlooking Puget Sound and smoke pot watching the ferries slug from one end to the other.

Steve lived on Charleston just off California and on the way to his house the road went practically vertical and then peaked and declined. If you ignore the warning signs and run that hill at fifty or sixty the car actually goes airborne and lands hard, still rolling down the hill at the bottom of which is a four-way stop. But at that speed, upon landing, you barrel right through the intersection.

During the summer between junior and senior years of high school Steve and I would swim in his pool almost daily. Steve was a phenomenal swimmer but rarely swam with others because he was self-conscious of the birthmark on his chest. It was huge, a dark discoloration that covered his pec and stretched into his stomach. It looked like a continent. Some days after swimming we'd retire to his bedroom and take turns playing the guitar for each other. Steve sang too. And he always wore a cap, usually turned backwards.

The same year I first saw Phish, Steve and I saw James Brown at The Paramount Theater. And it was amazing.

My Five Favorite Concerts:

5. The Trey Anastasio Band, Roseland Ballroom, New York, NY (2002)
4. Beck, The Keyspan Arena, Seattle, WA (2000)
3. Modest Mouse, The Showbox, Seattle, WA (2000)
2. Phish, The Star Lake Amphitheatre, Burgettstown, PA (2003)
1. James Brown, The Paramount Theater, Seattle, WA (1998)

At that concert Steve and I stood front and center at the foot of the stage not four feet from the Godfather himself. The man moved like a creature that had been to hell and back. He sang with spirit and lust, commanding the twelve-member band with a series of simple gestures. His presence commanded your full attention. He had a guitarist, bassist, full horn section, two drummers, three backup singers, five dancers, a magician for intermission, and of course, a man to bring out the cape.
 We were the only white people in the Theater and certainly the youngest but that didn't matter.
 James Brown screamed, sweat, shrieked, and stomped in front of me, so close that when he pushed his microphone out into the audience I thought it was falling on me until he tugged the cord sending it back to him, past him, when he dropped to his knees and caught it just before it hit the floor.
 It was spectacular
 And at the end of the concert, James Brown leaned over and shook my hand.

It was the best concert I have ever seen. The best concert I will ever see. The best concert any of you will ever fucking see.

Steve and I talked about that concert almost every time we saw each other, but it's just one of those experiences beyond description. Like love or a broken bone or your first blowjob. That's James Brown.

And if this book were a 1980s horror film it would now segue to a campfire circle in which my friends and I are roasting marshmallows or hot dogs and someone says, "Okay, cool. Now, Rob, what's the best concert you've ever gone to?" And Rob takes his turn but before he finishes we all hear a woman scream in the distance and leave to investigate, splitting up on the way, getting murdered one by one in unique and ghastly and horrific ways.

Camping is always a long party during which you never stop drinking, eat when you want, sleep when you want, and we brought drugs too. Someone was always coming or going and there was anywhere from five to twenty of us camping there throughout the week. We cooked BBQ ribs and fish from the river. One night the girls made a pasta dinner with salad and cake for dessert. A couple of days we went out boating and jet skiing in the Columbia River.

I could get those jet skis going eighty between pillars of the I-90 bridge. When a ski bucks you at that speed you skid across the water and by the time you realize what's happened you're underwater and your life-vest is pulling you to the surface. Damn we had fun with those machines. We raced across the river, probably two miles wide, and once or twice Mike and I played chicken.

He always flinched first. They were his father's jet skis.

At the end of the day two lucky individuals rode the skis back to the pier while the rest rode on the boat and one day Steve and I decided to go tandum on a ski to shore. The two girls riding the other ski took off and the boat followed before we even had our ski started. And it didn't take long to realize it wasn't going to start. But by that time both the girls and the boat were out of sight.

"Just give it a minute," I said. We needed to remain hopeful.

Steve and I laughed and joked.

"We're gonna die here, you know?" I said.

"I'm prepared to die," Steve said.

We occasionally tried and failed to start the jet ski.

"Next time, I promise," Steve said.

"It better," I said.

Then the joking stopped.

"Are we getting lower?" Steve asked.

The water, which was once at our ankles, had reached our calves. We were sinking.

To buy some time we jumped in the water and floated hopelessly. The jet ski continued to sink.

An hour passed.

"I'm really cold," Steve said.

I was shivering.

We were directly in the middle of the river with a mile swim to shore on either side of us. And the jet ski was half submerged. Why hadn't someone come back to look for us? How long would I wait on shore before sending out a rescue party?

Eventually, the jet ski went under and Steve and I laughed either because we had gone half-mad or because we had survived the jet ski.

Steve and I floated, waiting in silence.

It had been hours.

I was beginning to think awful, paranoid thoughts. Who knows what creatures live in this massive, incredibly deep river? We'd have to swim for it. And I wouldn't make it.

Steve blew the whistle attached to his life vest. He saw them first: a pair of jet skiers in the distance. Steve blew that whistle; he blew until his cold, gray face turned purple and red. Only just before he gave up, only as the skiers turned to go back the way they came, did they see us. During that moment, bobbing in the water watching them speed towards us, I felt like I was worth something. All the insignificance that saturates you hour after hour abandoned in a such a river, the almighty power of nature over humans, all that sank to the bottom.

They were both girls, our rescuers, one on a single-person jet ski, the other on a two-seater. "What are you guys doing?" the blonde asked.

"Waiting for you," Steve said.

They laughed and the brunette agreed to take one of us on her ski and the other one could hang on the back and get towed to shore. I climbed on that jet ski before Steve could even make a move. The girl's hair smelled like shampoo and I hugged tightly to her life vest as Steve clung to the rear of the ski.

As she drove us towards shore the river didn't seem like the death trap it once was. Suddenly, Steve howled and looking over my shoulder I saw that he had let go. We had driven over a shallow, rocky sandbar,

THE LAST AMERICAN GYPSY

dragging Steve's chest and stomach across the rocks. He stood knee-deep on the sandbar with a bloody chest, wincing but laughing too. I volunteered to stay behind, and she took Steve to the pier planning to come back for me.

I stood on the shallow sandbar in the middle of the river and watched them ride away and eventually out of sight. Standing by yourself in the middle of a river is humbling. No noise. No wind. No plants or animals. Just the river. And the sky. And all other forms of nature more powerful and vast than yourself.

But I didn't feel insignificant or irrelevant. I felt like a small piece of an unimaginably large structure that is planet earth or at least America. Meriwether Lewis and William Clark followed this river to the Pacific

Ocean on the last leg of their voyage. And now, some hundred years later, I stood the middle of it.

And the sun warmed my skin.

Tim arrived the next day, just in time for the show. We were camped at the base of this gravel mountain and Sparky and I climbed to the top with the intention of sliding down on a piece of cardboard or a shovel, both of which we carried to the peak with us. This was right around the time when I was making videos of myself in my dad's old army uniform, boots, Kevlar helmet, the works. And I wore the uniform for our climb. A small crowd gathered at the base of the mountain to see how this bearded soldier would descend and that's about the time when Tim arrived.

"I showed up and all these people were sitting drinking facing this mountain," Tim later said. "And then I heard someone say, 'Andy's gonna break his fucking neck,' so I knew I was in the right place."

The cardboard didn't really work as a sled and the shovel was no better.

I heard someone below yell, "Cartwheel! Cartwheel!"

"Don't disappoint your audience," Sparky said.

"You're right," I said and took a few steps back. With a running start I threw myself into a cartwheel and soared. I rolled and bounded down the mountain. Gravel and sky, gravel sky, gravel and sky, all the way, end over end… I lost all sense of self and placement. The momentum consumed me and in the middle of it there was a moment when I knew nothing before falling and nothing after falling. The fall was my existence. Then I came to rest.

And Phish tour is a lot like that. You gain a momentum going from show to show every day for weeks. You drink and party from morning into night and wake up the next day to do it all over again in a different town. In a sense the outside world disappears and when the tour is over and you return home the feeling is like coming out of a good film: the world is new and different because you had forgotten it for a moment.

I don't read newspapers on Phish tour. I don't watch television. I don't ride the subway. I don't cook dinner. I don't think about bills. I don't go to work. I don't wake up in my apartment with my alarm clock buzzing and my neighbors talking loudly. I don't use my keys to lock up before I leave.

When I returned from my travels this summer, basically ten weeks on the road, I came home and couldn't remember what key opened the front door to my building. It doesn't take long to remove yourself from the every day grind and now, sitting in my bedroom writing about my time on Phish tour, I can't help but miss that escape, that alternative to all this real life. Phish is no more, they broke up, and I have no problem with that.

It's their decision.

But that's not to say I don't miss it.

Last summer, after those two Gorge shows with Tim and my Seattle friends, I returned to Seattle and Tim drove to the next show in Salt Lake City. The next night I flew out of Seattle to Kansas City for a lay over on my way home to New York. Phish was scheduled to play The Verizon Amphitheatre in Boner Springs, Kansas after Salt Lake. Initially, I had planned to stay with Kai, but after the awkward, obligated hospitality with which she received me on my way out to Seattle, I checked-in to a hotel in Wyandotte county. I didn't even call her.

Kai lived in an old post office in the West Bottoms of Kansas City, Missouri that she and her friends had converted into a living space as well as an art gallery. The few days I stayed there on my way from New York to Seattle, she took me out to dinner and lunch and we visited a couple of art galleries but she often left me at the post office while she went out with her boyfriend who lived next door. I spent most of my time writing or lounging on the couch outside on the loading dock. I napped a lot too. And watched the trains come and go.

The post office was next to a train yard and almost every hour a train horn sounded loudly, eliminating all other sounds and thoughts in that hot, humid summer stagnation between what Kai and I had in New York and what we had then, which was much less.

I made good friends with her roommate Adam.

Adam was a nice tall, slender guy from South Carolina. He talked with that luke-warm Southern drawl and enjoyed beer as much as I do. One night while Kai was out with her boyfriend, Adam and I went gambling at the dog track. We didn't win a single race and drank until we were drunk, left, bought more beer, drove home, and drank warm Milwaukee's Best out on the loading dock with the nearby trains.

"We should just hop on one of those trains and ride it wherever it goes," I said.

"And then what?"

"Then we call Kai and have her come pick us up," I said, laughing.

"I can't do that, I have to work tomorrow," Adam said, laughing too. "I got to go feed spicy chicken wings to fat bitches all day tomorrow."

"Trust me," I said, talking louder and louder as a pair of trains crossed paths in the yard. "No one's gonna go hungry if you skip work tomorrow."

"What?" Adam asked, as the trains blew their horns and whistles and gained speed. We waited for the trains to pass. Then it was quiet again.

"Are we gonna do it or what?" I asked.

"No way," Adam said.

"Fine," I said, drunk and aggravated.

We continued to drink and the trains continued to roll through on their way to places like Chicago and St. Louis and points west.

So on my return layover in Kansas City, staying at a hotel, I had a day to kill before the concert and decided to spend it at the dog track.

I took a cab from the hotel.

My cab driver, Kamil, a well-mannered, warm-hearted Kurd from Iran argued with me about the price. We settled on a roundtrip fare and continued to chat during the drive. As he turned the car into the parking lot of The Woodlands racetrack he asked how long I planned on staying.

"Just a couple of hours," I said.

"Before ten?" He asked, eyes framed in the rearview mirror.

"Probably."

"Then maybe I join you?"

"Yeah, sure. Let's do it," I said, smiling.

Walking through the parking lot Kamil smoked an entire cigarette in two breaths. "I quit gambling, I quit, I say 'no more,'" he stammered nervously. "I even filled out the paper, it say 'I not allowed to bet anymore.' Maybe I just watch you bet."

"When did you quit?" I asked.

"Four months ago."

"I don't think they're gonna recognize you."

Kamil laughed and wrinkles spider-webbed from the corners of his eyes. "Probably not," he said.

Inside, I bought a soda and topped it off with the rum from my flask. Kamil bought a beer.

THE LAST AMERICAN GYPSY

"You got ice in your beer," I told him.
"I like it cold," Kamil replied with a mustache of foam.
"But you got *ice* in your fuckin' beer, man."
Kamil laughed and rubbed his bald spot.
We played the dogs all night long. We played the live races, the Jacksonville track, the buggies in Delaware, and every other simulcast racetrack. Kamil kept drinking beers with ice and I kept tipping the contents of my flask into my soda and when my flask was empty he bought me a beer with ice.
"Just try," he said.
Neither of us had won a race by eleven o'clock so we decided to bet on one more before leaving.

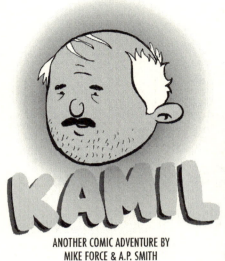

THE LAST AMERICAN GYPSY

"I meet her like I meet you. She passenger one night, crying about how she has nothing and no one and no place to go, so I say come to my place, I let her stay with me then I fall in love with the mother-bitch."

THE LAST AMERICAN GYPSY

"Okay. You find sex there maybe."

"Maybe," I said and we both laughed.

Kamil dropped me off at a bar called "Above The Hoop," a sports bar. I quickly made friends with the bartender and some locals and soon I was drinking for free. The bartender, some ugly, bitter woman, told me some dirty jokes and I told her some too, like the one about tampons.

"What did one tampon say to the other tampon?" I asked.

"Nothing," she said, knowing the joke. "They were both stuck up bitches."

The locals laughed and she poured everyone another round of some green concoction.

At the bar I made friends with some kids my age and they invited me to join them at their table near the PGA World Tour arcade game. In no time at all I was in the bathroom with my new friend Chico doing coke off the top of the urinal. He knew I was in town for Phish and wanted to talk about it. He'd seen Phish once.

"You should come to the show tomorrow," I said.

"I don't have a ticket," he said.

I shrugged my shoulders.

After Chico and his friends went home I found myself drinking with the bartender and two older gentlemen, the town's exterminator and the town's liquor store owner. We closed the bar and hours later, when we finally left, they took me to breakfast.

Eating pancakes and eggs, two other men joined us and we talked politics as the sun came up over the flatlands. They certainly had different opinions than I did but enjoyed listening to me and genuinely took in what I was saying. And I listened openly to them, which was a feat as drunk as I was. When the bill came I opened my wallet and remembered I had spent every last dollar at the dog track and when I explained that to the waitress she cut me short and told me to shut up before she made me wash dishes. Breakfast was on her.

"You're one lucky sonofabitch," the liquor store owner informed me.

"Thanks," I said.

"You need a ride to your hotel?" he asked.

"That'd be great," I slurred.

In the morning I woke up and stumbled in my boxers through the hotel to the hot tub. I soaked away my hangover, dressed, and wandered outside to see if I could find anyone on their way to the show. The parking lot was empty. I walked across the street to the other hotel and found a similar scene so I decided to hitch and walked a mile up the road to the freeway, made a sign that read PHISH, and stood near the entrance ramp.

It was damn hot that day. The sun was high in the sky and the air warmed your lungs with every breath. Cars and trucks drove past me and their drivers hardly glanced in my direction. None of them looked like they were going to the show.

It's easy to spot a Phish fan on tour, at gas stations and diners and rest areas. We all have a similar color scheme and posture: earthy, nomadic, relaxed, carefree. That day on the side of the freeway I saw only a few hippies drive past me. They avoided eye contact. Even on Phish tour, people are apprehensive about giving a stranger a ride.

I was once hitching a ride from Red Rocks back to where I was staying in Boulder after a Trey Anastasio show and this girl offered me a ride to the surprise of her boyfriend who didn't want to voice his opinion against her generosity. Waiting outside her car for traffic to die down I happily made small talk with the girl who shared her peanut butter and jelly, post-show sandwich while her boyfriend eyed me suspiciously from his seat on the trunk of the car. Then, after he insisted upon taking my backpack and putting it in the car, he pulled out an apple and said, "I hate to eat it without cutting it, you don't have a KNIFE do you?"

pocket knife

"No, I don't have a knife," I said.

"Really? Not even a pocket KNIFE?"

"No," I said.

But after the ride back to Boulder he gave me a hug and I felt like I may have influenced his view of strangers or hitchhikers or perhaps people in general. I know it's not the sixties but I don't think there's any more risk in giving a stranger a ride these days than there was in that decade. Especially to and from a Phish concert. And in my experience, Colorado is the easiest place to hitch. Much easier than Kansas.

I waited sweating next to that freeway in Bonner Springs for close to forty minutes before a gray Acura Integra with three riders pulled over.

"Hop in," the passenger said. The three of them, all in their late twenties, seemed like gentle people and I felt no bad vibes, that is to say I sensed that they only wanted to help me out. It's important when hitchhiking, to a Phish concert or otherwise, to be prepared to make split second first impression judgment calls. I refuse to carry a weapon so I rely solely on my instinct.

"You making the whole run?" the driver asked after we made our introductions.

"Not really," I said. "I saw The Gorge, making it back to New York after this."

"Yeah, we saw The Gorge shows too," the shotgun rider said. "They were a little mellow."

"Yeah, they could have been better."

"Could have been a better set list," said the guy next to me in the backseat.

"Definitely," I said. "You guys making the whole run?"

"We had planned to but something came up and we're just doing Gorge through Alpine."

"That's decent enough."

"Yeah," the driver said.

"Well," my backseat companion said, then paused. "We were gonna do the whole run but my parents died in a plane crash in Alaska so I have to go to the funeral."

The car seemed to slow.

"Jesus, man, I'm sorry," I said. I felt like touching the kid. "That's terrible."

"Yeah, it was just a small four-passenger plane and they went through a cloud and flew straight into a mountain," he explained. "The search party didn't find them for five days."

We hit traffic almost immediately.

When we finally reached the lot and parked all of us stood around the car smoking a joint and I introduced them to the Orgasmatron, a head massager I bought on the Internet when I was sixteen years old. The Orgasmatron is made of six copper, soft-tipped prongs branching out from a handle. Using the appropriate amount of teasing twisting plunging on your head, it feels like a beautiful female Goddess is washing your hair with long, manicured fingernails. At Phish shows and gatherings where hippies commune, it is an instant friend-maker as well as an occasional source of income. Donations only, of course.

Someone first introduced me to The Orgasmatron at The Gorge during set break at a Phil and Friends/Bob Dylan show I went to with Allison, my girlfriend at the time. We were lounging, stoned on the grassy hill in the sun when this man wearing a poncho and an African hat approached Allison and asked if she'd like to try the Orgasmatron. She looked at me for approval or assurance and I said, "Yeah, baby, give it a try."

The man stepped behind her and told me to "watch her face," as he plunged this device down on her head. She loved it, immediately closing her eyes, parting her lips. In the middle of the massage she let out an rapturous moan.

It gave her goose bumps.

"My turn," I told the hippie.

He did me and I was hooked, sold, completely enamored by the device, the Orgasmatron. I bought one as soon as I got home and it arrived in four weeks. All my friends loved it and I was reminded to bring it to every party, especially every rave. At music festivals and concerts people would give me money, drugs, booze, jewelry, hugs, and kisses for massaging them with the Orgasmatron.

But that was seven years ago and things have changed since then.

I don't bring the Orgasmatron with me on tour anymore because without fail someone's uncle, cousin, sister, or brother "has one of those!" And "Aren't those things amazing!"

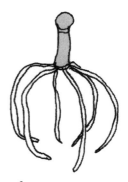

the orgasmatron

These days at such festivals and concerts, vendors actually sell the apparatus under names like Brain Scrambler, Mind Tingler, and Spiritual Massager. You can buy an Orgasmatron through *Sky Mall* magazine on airplanes and I once heard that Katie Couric brought one out on *The Today Show*.

But that day in Bonner Springs, the Orgasmatron came in real handy. Not only did it function as a thank you for the boys who drove me to the show, but I made a few bucks and got a few joints in the lot just walking around asking people if they'd like to try it. Usually, people at Phish concerts are more inclined to try something called the Orgasmatron than people elsewhere. And I've heard a million references to both the 1998 film *Orgasmatron* as well as Woody Allen's *Sleepers*.

That Kansas show was the last show to which I brought the Orgasmatron. Because of that Midwestern heat and the general exhaustion of those who drove from eastern Washington through Utah to be there, the Orgasmatron was a welcomed experience. I even traded a massage for a T-shirt this cute girl was pushing. Her shirts were canary yellow and in black text read, IT'S DAMN HOT! I almost fell in love with her.

Inside the venue, at set break, I caught up with Tim and some friends of ours who hailed from Rochester and we danced through the second set. At the end of the show Tim drove me back to my hotel room and in the parking lot I helped him plan his route for the overnight drive to Indiana.

"You sure you don't want to just come with?" Tim asked, holding a map.

"I should get on that flight tomorrow."

"You sure?"

The next day I flew home to New York. Sparky and Dylan had flown out to visit me and were waiting for me with Sam at my apartment by the time I arrived. They came mostly to see me and visit the city but planned their trip around The Siren Music Festival, the annual Coney Island festival thrown by *The Village Voice*. Modest Mouse was headlining that year.

But The Siren Festival sucked: too many people, too many poseurs, too many stages. Modest Mouse played to an indifferent audience who applauded at inappropriate times. It was obvious that the band was dispirited by the crowd and didn't even play an encore. It made me miss Phish and somewhat regret not hopping in the car with Tim in Kansas.

But Sparky and Dylan and I had fun throughout the week and when they left, in fact the very day they left, I met Eric and Adam at a bar for drinks and thoughtlessly asked Adam if he wanted to rent a car and drive down to North Carolina to catch the Phish shows there and meet up with some friends who would then drive us through the rest of the tour back to New York.

"Okay," he said.

"Really?"

"Sure."

So the next day we rented a car and drove to Greensboro, North

Carolina where my friend Laura lived. I drove all thirteen hours and during the last leg, through thick pine-lined hills, the road moved like a treadmill.

But we made it and drank until dawn with Laura on her back porch.

When Laura and I were fourteen we spent many Saturday nights by the side of her pool drinking her grandfather's booze and smoking his cigars. One moonless night I would have drowned had Laura not pulled my drunk-ass out of the deep end. Even then Laura was a good guitarist, and a great singer. Now she plays gigs at bars and coffee shops and is doing well as a folk rock singer in the South.

The first show we hit on that run was in Charlotte. Decent enough show, of what I remember. Bezer was obsessed with finding mushrooms for the show so we split up in the lot and later found each other during set break. Actually, I think that was the Raleigh show. Or maybe it was Charlotte. Sometimes the shows blend together. Wait, I remember now. Laura and I lost Bezer *during* set break because he went looking for mushrooms and we never saw him again.

After the show, back at the car Laura and I drank a beer waiting for Bezer. And then another beer. Slowly the lot cleared out and our car was one of only a few remaining.

A cop rolled by in a golf cart and told us to get moving.

"Officer," I said. "If my friend was sick or arrested where would I go to find out?"

"Did he have any drugs on him?" the cop asked.

"Probably," I said.

"Well, we arrested two hundred people tonight," the cop said. "Better to go home and see if he calls in the morning."

Then he sped off in his police golf cart.

Laura was concerned but I had faith. A small amount of faith, but faith nonetheless. Bezer would find the car eventually. And he did. Wide-eyed and smiling. He'd finally found his mushrooms.

"But I don't think they're working," he said.

"Well, how long ago did you eat them?"

"Maybe twenty minutes? I also ate a tab of acid that I think I got ripped off for."

"Let me see the mushrooms."

He reached into his camouflage cargo shorts, his Phish tour uniform, and pulled out a handful of dried, blue-veined mushrooms.

"Those look real enough," I told him.

"Will you try some?"

"Sure," I said eating a small handful as the three of us piled into the car.

We drove mostly in silence through backwoods roads past signs warning of deer and sharp curves. At some point Bezer let out an unexpected giggle. Then he took a flash photo that temporarily blinded me at the wheel.

"Jesus, man!" I said. "Don't be taking pictures in the car!"

Laura glared at me suspiciously.

"He didn't take a picture," Laura said.

"I didn't take a picture," Bezer said.

The three of us laughed. We laughed all the way back to Laura's house as I concentrated on avoiding the psychedelic deer I imagined leaping out in front of the car.

Back at the house, I ate some more mushrooms, Bezer did too, and Laura went to bed, and Bezer and I watched back-to-back episodes of *Cops* on Court TV. Every single suspect in every single episode had either a gun, a crack rock, or both.

Bezer ate another handful and put on the movie *Spiderman*.

The sun was rising, and I fell asleep right around the time Willem DaFoe turned into the Green Goblin.

In the morning I stepped out onto Laura's back porch for a cigarette and to call my mom, let her know I was in North Carolina. On the phone, telling her about the brutal thirteen-hour drive, I looked down at my bare feet. In permanent marker on my left and right feet respectively, read the words: LEFT and RIGHT.

Bezer slept in late that day, which was fine because we had planned to skip the show in Atlanta that night and instead drive out to the coast, out to Wilmington, where Bezer's childhood friend David lived with his pregnant wife and a few Marine Corps buddies.

We rolled into Wilmington around nine or ten and drank three beers instantly. David and his friends were thrilled to see Bezer and it was good to see Bezer happy among these life-long pals.

David's wife was pregnant as all hell, ready to pop at any minute.

"What do you guys want to do tonight?" David asked us. He was shirtless and muscular, perfect smile, the kind of guy who got laid every weekend in high school.

We were sitting on his front porch in a neighborhood, both residential and sprawling. Coming from New York, or even Greensboro, these houses were really, really far apart.

"There's a party about three houses down," one of the Marines said. He was also shirtless. They all were.

The party was in someone's enormous backyard, hosted by a local but thrown by a crew of  *Jackass*-types who drive an RV across the country stopping here and there, setting up, buying a few kegs, and once everyone gets drunk, they start paying people to do stupid things on camera. There must have been three hundred people there.

Some cameraman offered me fifty dollars to let a girl punch me in the face.

"Only if she's wearing a cowboy hat," I told the cameraman. "And she has to be shorter than me."

Off he went to find someone who matched my description.

I'd lost Bezer at the party almost immediately and when he found me he slipped a gram of cocaine into my pocket. "We're sharing that with David," he told me.

In the bathroom I did almost the whole gram and later when Bezer requested it I told him it was gone and he didn't care, had already done a gram himself and went back for another three, one of which he gave me, before running off again.

I poured myself a beer at one of the many kegs and flirted with some girls but everyone was way too drunk for conversation, including myself. We'd only been in town for forty-five minutes and already I was flying high on a beer-soaked carpet ride.

I poured myself another beer and noticed that a crowd had formed in the distance and I pushed my way to the front. In center of this crowd a girl sat in a chair holding a bottle of vodka and a man kneeled next to her with his head on her lap. The man started digging into his eye and then plucked out his eyeball, a glass eye.

Then the girl poured some vodka into his open eye cavity, bent over, and sucked it out.

The crowd roared and one of the cameramen gave both the drinker and the vessel a hundred dollar bill.

I was impressed.

Back to the keg.

I found some of those shirtless Marine buddies and we chatted about Iraq. I stood there with four or five of these muscular soldiers, all of whom had USMC tattooed on their biceps. I had dreadlocks, a large beard, and a beer belly.

We knew each other's standpoints on the war, that was not up for discussion, and we made an unspoken agreement not to attempt any persuasion. We talked about the war like people talk about their hometowns. One soldier couldn't wait to go back. One soldier never got sent and felt left out. And the others were happy to be alive and excited to talk about their experiences. A Marine named Jack showed me his scars.

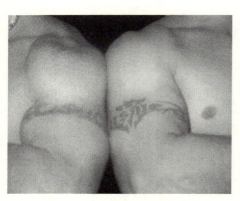

Marines

"This is where the bullet entered," he said, pointing to his arm just above his elbow. "This is where it exited," he said, showing me the other side. "Then it entered here," pointing at his chest, "and it exited again here," pointing to a round discoloration on his back.

"I don't know if we're doing anything better for those people," one Marine said. "But it sure is a rush out there."

"Oh, the biggest adrenaline rush you can imagine," another said. "They shoot at you, you shoot right back."

"Isn't that scary?" I asked.

"Well," one Marine said, looking at his buddies. "You just never know if you're going to make it through the day, you know?"

The others nodded.

Back to the keg.

I'm standing there, pouring beers for cute girls, pouring myself a few in the meantime, drinking, chatting it up, having a good time. Bezer walks up to me and says to get away from the keg because "I think the cops are here."

"Don't worry," I said.

Then this older guy wearing a visor walked past and casually pointed at me saying, "him."

Suddenly I'm on the ground. My face is in the mud and I've got a knee on my back, my hands pinned behind me then cuffed and I'm standing again, handcuffed and being pushed through the crowd, some of whom were making a run for it. There were cops everywhere and I was freaking out.

"What the fuck!" I screamed, as my arresting officer pushed me though the throng. "Why the fuck am I being arrested! What the fuck is this!" I screamed viciously all the way through the backyard to the front of the house where there were eight police cruisers, two ambulances, and one paddy wagon. It was quite a sight.

"Why the fuck am I being arrested!" I screamed.

The cop pulled down hard on my handcuffs and I fell back against his chest.

"Why the fuck am I being arrested!"

"Because you got long hair, dirty hippie," the cop told me.

Then he threw me into the paddy wagon.

I stumbled to my knees, stood up, and sat on the cold bench across from the only other person in the wagon: an ugly, skinny bald kid wearing only a gold necklace and a red Speedo.

"What're you in for?" he asked me.

"Having long hair," I said. "You?"

"Wearing a Speedo."

We sat laughing quietly as the cops periodically opened the door to throw in someone else. I'm sure had we not been handcuffed we would have helped up those poor sonsofbitches but no one made a move and most everyone was quiet except one who bitched and complained until someone wiser told him to "shut the fuck up!"

It was right about then, sitting with half a dozen drunkards in the paddy wagon, that I remembered the cocaine in my pocket.

For a moment I thought I'd just ride it out and see what happens. There was no way I could reach my front pocket. Maybe if I asked someone else to dig in my front pocket, they could pull it out and just toss it on the floor? That might work.

The wagon door opened and two officers stood there pointing at me. "You," one said. "Get up."

Everyone in the wagon looked at me with equal amounts envy and pity.

Outside the wagon I stood handcuffed facing a trio of stocky law enforcement officers. These men, these Southerners, these men were men of the law. And the red and blue oscillating lights only magnified that atmosphere. Looking about, I saw there was no place to run.

"You got ID, son?"

"Yes, I do."

"Let's see it."

"Can you un-cuff me?"

"No, we'll just pull it out for you," the cop said. "It's in your back pocket?"

I nodded, happy they were starting at the back. While he riffled through my wallet, I directed him to my military ID instead of my Washington state driver's license.

"Whatya think?" one cop asked the other.

"Were you pouring beer for people?" the cop asked me.

"I was pouring beer for myself," I lied.

"It's okay if you poured yourself a beer and then some for a few friends."

He was trying to trick me. "But I didn't," I said.

"You just poured beer for yourself?"

"Yes."

"No one else?"

"Yes."

The three stared at me. I had a difficult time focusing and my throat was filling with cocaine phlegm. The drip.

"Well, whatya think?" one cop asked the other.

"Whatayou think?"

"I don't think he's a part of it," the other answered, eyeing me for some kind of sign, twitch or a movement that would say otherwise. I didn't even blink.

"Okay, we're gonna let you go," the cop said. "Turn around."

They unlocked my handcuffs and I walked. I walked slowly, concentrating on each step. And I never looked back.

Back at David's house, Bezer, David, and all the Marines greeted me with warm smiles and high-fives and back slaps and bear hugs. They were thrilled to see me. For a moment I felt like I too was a Marine back from Iraq.

"We were talking to the cops for you the whole time!" Jack told me. "Each one of us went up one at a time and told them you had nothing to do with this and that you were a friend of ours who had only been in town for forty-five minutes."

I was grateful beyond words so we shared a few more back slaps and high-fives before heading inside.

We stayed inside for the rest of the evening finishing the cocaine and just after sunrise Adam and I passed out on the floor in the living room. That afternoon David, his wife, Adam and I ate breakfast at a diner called Whitey's where, history tells us, Michael Jordan worked as a cook before going to college at the University of North Carolina.

Then Bezer and I drove back west from the coast towards Greensboro to pick up Laura and her friend Kenny before heading back east to Raleigh for the show. The drive to Greensboro was long and tedious. My vision was lacking and my head throbbed and the traffic was miserable. At one point, Bezer became really annoyed with the woman in a white Lexus tailgating us at seventy miles an hour.

I tapped the breaks a few times, but she never relented.

"Fuck this," Bezer said, rolling down the window. He opened his V8 juice, red and creamy, looked back at the Lexus, then out the window, then back at the Lexus, then suddenly he tossed the juice out the window. Red paste covered her windshield and the Lexus swerved, breaking, and then the windshield wipers cleaned the juice off. Bezer laughed loudly, proud of his success.

I looked at him disapprovingly.

"Oh, fuck that bitch," he said. "She shouldn't tailgate."

"But you blinded her, she could have crashed."

"Whatever. Fuck her. Just don't let her pass us."

I didn't. I kept us speeding away from Wilmington, straight through Raleigh, back to Greensboro where we picked up Kenny and Laura, returned our rental car, and then I drove Laura's jalopy back towards

Raleigh. About thirty miles out, traffic stopped. No one was moving.

We were behind schedule and Laura grew anxious because none of us had tickets. I rolled down my window and stuck my finger in the air. Two minutes later, a pair of guys in a corvette yelped at us. They had two extra tickets and we bought them for face, exchanging cash for tickets from car to car. Then Laura stuck her finger out her window and two minutes later a pair of girls in a pick-up yelped at us. They had two extra tickets and we bought them for face, exchanging cash for tickets from car to car.

Almost immediately traffic subsided and we rolled gracefully towards the venue.

In the lot I ate some mushrooms and we walked around to try and buy some better pot than what we had already and found not a single dealer, vendor, no one was selling anything and the cops were everywhere. Cops on horseback, cops with nightsticks, Raleigh cops, state cops, typically obvious undercover cops. Everywhere. And the vibe in the lot was one of anger. People felt persecuted.

And there were hundreds of fingers in the air.

Near the gates to the venue I watched a man fall and puke all over himself. He thrashed about on the ground in his own puddle for a few minutes before the cops circled him and a medic golf cart rolled up. A crowd gathered to watch. He put up a decent fight, puked on one of the medics, took a swing at the air, but then they strapped him to the stretcher and he stopped struggling, probably passed out.

"Hey, give us his ticket!" someone in the crowd screamed.

"Why can't you just leave him alone?" someone else yelled.

"Give me his ticket!"

"Give us his ticket!"

"Give me his ticket!"

"Yeah, give us his ticket!"

THE LAST AMERICAN GYPSY

PART THREE

The Purple Cape of a Man Named Juice
&
The Illegal Underbelly of Camp Close By

Near Saratoga Springs, New York, Lee's Campground is something of a legend: a lakefront grassland that accommodated hundreds of thousands of hippies and vagabonds throughout the career and tours of The Grateful Dead and then Phish.

The Grateful Dead was Vince Welnick, Mickey Hart, Bill Krutzman, Bob Weir, Phil Lesh, and Jerry Garcia. They met and first played together in San Francisco in the early 1960s.

Phish was Mike Gordon, Jon Fishman, Page McConnell, and Trey Anastasio. They met and first played together in at The University of Vermont in the early 1980s.

Twenty years apart, but certainly their tours overlapped in the years before 1995, when Jerry Garcia died on August ninth.

On August 9th, 1995, I was living in North Carolina and my father and I spent that afternoon staining the back deck of the house. I spent a lot of time in that football field of a backyard we had in North Carolina. I picked up pinecones as a chore, then cut the grass, played soccer, read, wrote, and I did it all listening to tapes of The Grateful Dead on a tired, old boom box. And that afternoon staining the deck was no exception. But when the tape ended, instead of finding another, I tuned to the local classic rock station.

"We can take a break," my dad says. "I'm gonna go to the store."

But I continued painting on that stain listening to CCR and The Doors and then I heard the DJ speak: "I just received news that, early this morning, Jerry Garcia died of an apparent heart attack in his room at the Forest Knolls Drug Rehabilitation Center. We'll miss you Jerry."

Then the DJ played "Playing With The Band," and the opening notes turned that hot, humid August air dry and chilly.

When my father returned, beer in hand, he stopped short of the deck and stood for a moment in the doorway. He looked wounded.

"Were you listening to the radio?" he asked.

"Yeah," I said, wiping the sweat from my forehead. I sighed.

"Come inside," he said. "We're done for the day."

We sat in the kitchen and he told me his story of when he went to the Watkins Glen concert as a teenager and saw The Band and The Dead. He told the story somberly, with imposed excitement. It sounded like a eulogy.

I never saw The Grateful Dead play.

And three years after Garcia's death, September '98, I saw my first Phish concert at The Gorge.

But that wasn't when I was introduced to the tour scene.

Once, when I was in the sixth grade, my class took a field trip to the Seattle Center for some science fair. What the science fair organizers didn't consider was that The Grateful Dead was playing the Seattle Center that evening. So that afternoon my friends and I skipped out on the science fair and wandered amongst these long-haired, free-talking, drum-beating, all-smiles people. And even then, as a young teen, I appreciated their lifestyle, their community. The colored vans, the long-haired twirling women, the bearded drumming elderly, the variety of smells, the warmth of the crowd, the smiles everyone shined down upon me...

I knew one day I would ride with a tribe like this.

Ten years later, the night I stayed at Lee's Campgrounds in Saratoga was the last night anyone would camp there during a weekend of Phish concerts.

And everyone was up and howling.

We had a blast.

But like war, a long, drug-infested party harvests only bodies when the smoke clears, and just after sunrise, I stumbled around blessing the bodies of the dead like a priest on the battlefield. It seemed like there were hundreds of dead or sleeping boys and girls.

Those nights, those parties, those shows, the beginning of the last, were all that they could have been. Looking back at it, most of those two weeks have melted together and all I remember is a few sets, a couple of excellent jams here and there, this town and that town, and the omnipresent hiss of thirty nitrous-oxide tanks throughout a dimly lit campground near dawn and then into morning. Sometimes you fail to notice the sunrise. Sometimes you sleep through it, and sometimes it sneaks right past you.

I remember one sunrise specifically, but it wasn't at Lee's. The sunrise I'm remembering was at Camp Close By in Indiana. Tim and I rolled into Indiana from Pennsylvania via Ohio late that night/early morning, took the exit we remembered and followed the homemade signs leading us into the campground. At the entrance, a speakfreak, wide-eyed thirty-something with a flashlight searched our car, "not for drugs or anything like that," he said. "This is a hassle-free campground. Hassle-free," he repeated. "I just wanna make sure you aren't sneaking in your friends. It's thirty bucks each for the weekend."

We paid, he gave us our campsite bracelets and a parking permit to keep on the dashboard, and we rolled into camp. We could hear the nitrous tanks hissing already and as soon as we set up our tent, we made ourselves a drink, I bought a balloon, and we introduced ourselves to the neighboring gypsy hippies.

One of the unique and enjoyable aspects of Camp Close By is the fact that, unlike most campsites, parking and camping are in separate areas. This allows for a more natural camp setting and eliminates the blockades and obstructions that befall when a few hundred hippies camp amongst their cars, vans, caravans.

Tim and I stayed up all night drinking with our new friends and after Tim went to sleep I befriended a man with a sixty-gallon nitrous tank and we huffed straight from the hose until dawn when the reverberating WAWAWAAWAWAWAAA of the nitrous eating my brain hushed and stopped and I passed out in a neighbor's lawn chair.

In my sleep I felt a gentle hand rubbing my thigh. I opened my eyes and saw the dark purple sky in its warming period just before baby blue, and looking down, I found a pretty, teenage face of a blonde girl smiling up at me from the ground and rubbing my leg.

"Good morning," she said.

"Morning," I replied.

Then she handed me a balloon full almost to bursting with nitrous. I sucked it down and during the ensuing WAWA she stood up, leaned into me, and kissed me on the lips, a soft, sensual slow kiss.

Then she trotted off and the WAWAWA abated and I closed my eyes again for sleep.

"Wandering" or "roaming" are words often used by gypsy-oppressors when describing the gypsy lifestyle. And it's always in a negative tone. These words imply aimlessness, as if gypsy lives have no purpose or direction. But in reality, the lifestyle of the gypsies is quite purposeful, and at the very least a determined course built around community, travel, storytelling, and music if only because that lifestyle is rarely supported in the more traditional, contemporary societies.

But what most of these gypsy-oppressors don't consider is the harsh reality of conditions of a life on the road, the day-to-day responsibilities of feeding a family, or feeding oneself, or just generally making money.

On the June '04 Phish run I came across a few unexpected expenditures. I had not had the beer turn-over I had hoped for. What I mean to say is that I drank more beer than I sold and then bought enough nitrous balloons to run my wallet dry. I needed to make some quick cash. And at Camp Close By I came across an excellent opportunity.

A friend named Jay, this Amish-looking red-head from Red Bank, New Jersey, some kid I'd known only from tour, but known for over a year, well, I'd heard at Lee's in Saratoga that this guy had a lot of pot he wanted to sell. Apparently Jay had pounds and pounds of this shit, or so claimed this burn-out in Saratoga. And at the rate he wanted to sell it, I could bag it up into eighths of an ounce and flip it in the campsite and make a few hundred bucks that would bring me well out of the hole.

That afternoon at Camp Close By I went on a mission to find Jay and soon enough I ran into a friend of his who said he was staying at a different site but was coming by Camp Close By in a little bit and that "he has a shit load of pot if you're looking to score."

"Yeah, maybe," I said. "I'll come find you later on."

In the meantime I walked around asking for pot just to kind of feel out the demand. Most people I passed at camp said, "No, but if you find some let me know." I remembered where those people were camped and went back to my camp where I found Tim and Jay and a few others circled around a bong.

"Hey, dude," I said to Jay.

"Hey, man," he said. "My buddy told me you were looking for work."

"Yeah, well, let's talk," I said.

So Jay and I left and walked to the other side to camp where we climbed into his buddy's tent. From a rolled up sleeping bag Jay procured a gallon size bag of pot, something like half a pound from the looks of it.

"It's not the best herb in the world," Jay said. "In fact, it's beasters, but you shouldn't have any trouble getting rid of it, no one around here is holding."

"Yeah, so how much are you looking for?"

"Well," Jay started, and it was obvious he was trying to be bigger than he was. He wasn't used to selling this much pot at once, but, on the other hand, I wasn't used to buying this much. Slowly we worked out a deal and, if all went well, I stood to make a few hundred bucks.

"Okay, so how much money can you give me now?" Jay asked.

"Nothing," I said. "That's why I need the work."

Jay looked confused. Then angry. "You mean you want me to give you a pound on the cuff?"

"Yeah," I said. "It's not like I'm going anywhere. I'll be here all weekend, then Wisconsin after that."

"And you think you can push it all before then?"

"No problem," I said.

"Okay," Jay said, skeptically. "Whatever you say. But I don't have it all here, we'll have to go back to my site to get the rest."

"Well, I'll just take what you have here."

"I don't have my scale," Jay said. "We need to go to my site to weigh it anyway."

Now I was the skeptical one.

"Maybe Tim can drive us," I said.

"Sure."

So we went back to my tent and I asked Tim to drive us and he was leery but agreed anyway. I said I'd smoke him out when we got back.

The plan was to drive up to the edge of Jay's site where he would jump out, grab the gear, jump in, and we would drive back to Camp Close By where we'd weigh it and I'd bag it.

And everything was working as planned, we already had the weight and were heading back to Close By when Tim missed the turn and made this quick, screeching U-turn in the middle of the road.

My testicles shrunk into my stomach.

"What the fuck was that?" Jay yelled from the backseat.

"Jesus, Tim," I said.

"Stop the car," Jay yelled. "Stop the car, I'm outta here!"

"Don't stop the fucking car, Tim," I said. "Just keep driving."

"What's the big deal?" Tim asked.

"What's the big deal!" Jay yelped. "YOU DON'T FLIP A BITCH WITH A POUND OF WEED IN THE CAR!"

"It's fine, Jay," I said. "Just be cool."

"Whatever, you guys are assholes," Jay said.

We rode the rest of the way in fearful silence.

But we made it back to the site, without further incident, and we parked in the lot and weighed and bagged the pound.

"So that's six grand you owe me, buddy," Jay said.

"What?" I asked.

"Six. Six for the pound."

"Now, this isn't what we talked about," I said.

"Listen, I'm no idiot," Jay said. "I'm helping *you* out, not the other way around. It's six, take it or leave it."

"Then I'm leaving it," I said. "Fuck you. If you don't want to push all this at once, and have me doing all the work for you then fuck off. I'm sorry, dude, but I *am* helping you out."

Tim stayed out of it and Jay was silent for a moment.

"Alright," Jay said. "Let's say you're selling eighths for sixty. That's 128 eighths, which is…"

"6,100," I said.

"Okay…" Jay said.

"No," Tim said. "That's 7,680."

I glared at Tim.

"Exactly," Jay said. "So I'm cutting you a deal."

"Listen, you know as well as I that I'm not gonna get sixty an eighth for this pot. I'll be lucky to get forty, more like thirty, so let's say an even thirty-five hundred."

I stared at Tim so he kept his mouth shut.

"And let's not forget that you probably got this pound for twenty-eight hundred," I said.

Judging by Jay's blank-stare reaction, I was right.

"Fine," he said. "You owe me thirty-five hundred."

"Deal," I said.

So I stashed the pot in our tent and we drove Jay back to his site and on our way back to Camp Close By, Tim suddenly tensed and said a somber, "fuck."

"What?" I asked, but I already knew.

We were getting pulled over.

Not that we had anything in the car, maybe only whatever we each had in our pockets–and all I had were a few used balloons–but the car reeked like pot. When you break up a pound into 128 little baggies, the smell tends to linger.

Tim pulled over and the cop approached the car.

"What can I do for you, officer?" Tim asked.

"Get out of the car please, sir," said the cop.

"Sure," Tim said.

"You too," said the cop.

"Alright," I said.

Standing there on the side of the road, only yards from Camp Close By, the cop got straight to the point:

"I watched this car come by here just one too many times this afternoon, what are you boys selling?"

I laughed.

"You think this is funny, son?" the cop said. "I can smell the marijuana from here, you wouldn't object to us getting the dogs out here to go through your car, would you?"

"Not at all, sir," Tim said.

"Excuse me?" asked the cop.

"I said, not at all, sir," Tim said.

"Okay, let's stop all this fooling 'round here," said the cop. "May I

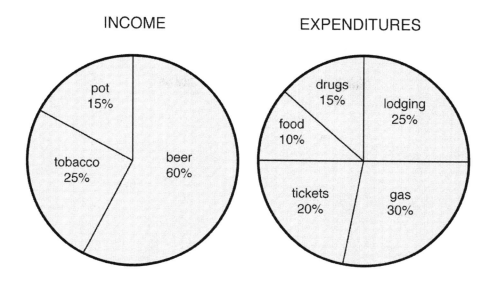

INCIDENT REPORT

11/30/99. Pepper sprayed, eluded arrest at WTO riots. Seattle, WA.
08/30/01. Interrogated, detained, accused of transporting contraband. Detroit, MI
01/24/01. Detained, issued a summons for subway fare evasion. New York, NY
01/05/02. Detained, strip searched by airport police. Norfolk, VA.
08/16/02. Interrogated, car searched by Canadian police. WA/B.C. border
03/20/03. Eluded arrest during the the Iraq War protest. New York, NY
06/12/03. Issued a court summons for open container. New York, NY
07/23/03. Cuffed, thrown, detained in police van. Willmington, NC
11/26/03. Detained and questioned about video footage. Celebration, FL
06/13/04. Cuffed to fence alongside I-90 for a while. Manchester, TN
06/20/04. Warned by undercover for selling pot. Deer Creek, IN
07/28/04. Interrogated at gunpoint by MPs and SS. Boston, MA
08/09/04. Arrested for selling liquor without a liquor licence. Norfolk, VA
08/11/04. Detained for selling cigarettes. Mansfield, MA

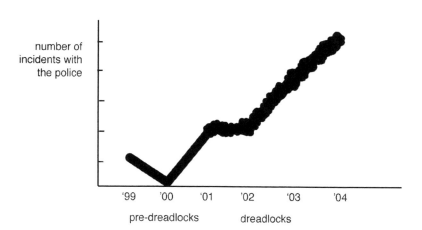

search your vehicle?"

"No," Tim said.

"Boys, I've got you. You're caught. And I'm gonna find that marijuana whether I search the vehicle or the dogs search your vehicle."

"But we don't have any pot," Tim said. "We just dropped off the last of it."

I thought I misheard Tim.

"You did what?" the cop asked.

"I said we just dropped it off. That's why the car still smells," Tim said.

"Well, where did you drop it off?"

"I don't know, one of those camps over there, maybe Bear Camp or Dancing Bear Camp...?"

"I think it was Big Bear Camp," I said.

The cop was stunned. They didn't teach this in cop school.

"Are you lying to me?" asked the cop.

"No, sir," we said in unison.

The cop hesitated. He poked his head through the window into the car. Then pulled out and stared at us for a moment.

"If I see this car on the road again," he threatened. "I *will* search it."

"Okay," Tim said.

"Now, get," said the cop.

Back at Camp Close By I rolled a joint the length of my arm and the width of my waist and Tim and I smoked it from one end to the other. And we laughed at the police.

Then I donned my uniform– black cowboy hat and aviator sunglasses–and got to work. I walked through the campsite, stopping at every pair, group, or family sitting outside their tents.

"You guys don't need any herb do you?" I ask.

"Actually," says the leader of the pack, "we were just looking for some."

"You guys need any pot?" I ask.

"Yes," a woman replies, "why yes we do."

"Lookin' for weed?" I ask.

"Let's see what you got," says a teenager pretending to know the difference between good pot and the garbage pot I was pushing.

But the quality doesn't matter.

People are happy to buy weed from a seasoned Phish-head with long dreads, a cowboy hat, and appropriately over-sized aviator sunglasses.

I sold the eighths for forty, and fifty when I could, that is to say when the buyer was naïve or desperate or wealthy. And in two hours I had over two thousand dollars in my back pocket.

Back at the tent, Tim was still smoking.

"How'd you do?" he asked.

"Pretty well, sold almost half of it," I said.

"Damn," said Tim. He was obviously intrigued. "Did you hit the whole campsite?"

"Pretty much," I said. "But I don't think I went all the way to the entrance area."

"Well, maybe, if you want, I'll take some and go for a walk that way."

"Sure," I said, and dug out a few eighths for Tim and then he left.

I was alone, sitting in the chair, contemplating where I should hide my two thousand. A pair of cute, dreadlocked girls came strutting towards me carrying four nitrous balloons each.

"Hey, sweetie," I called. "Can I have one of those?"

"Sure, baby," the uglier one said, and gave me a balloon without breaking her stride.

I sat sipping on the balloon, just casually, nothing overboard.

"Hey, dude?"

I turned and answered in a low, nitrous-induced voice, "Yeeaaaah?"

"We're making some drinks over here, you want a whiskey and coke?"

"Surrre," I said, standing, walking over.

The very first time I smoked pot I didn't get high. I smoked only a handful of times in the coming years, and didn't get high those times either.

The very first time I smoked pot *and* got high was May 16th, 1997. I was living in North Carolina, but moving to Seattle the next day. My father had been in Seattle for a few weeks and my mother and I hung around until I finished the school year. May 16th was the last day of school, my last day in North Carolina, and after school my friend Jenny, the very girl who introduced me to Phish, took me on a drive in her station wagon through the cotton fields and tobacco fields of North Carolina and smoked me out with a bamboo pipe.

I remember going to a diner in Roland, some one street-light town, and I was so high I couldn't understand a word anyone was saying and Jenny translated for the waitress.

Then we drove just a little farther to South Of The Border where we took the elevator to the top of the sombrero and while I urinated off the top, looking below at the matchstick cars of I-95, the wind changed direction and I watched my stream of piss curl out and sprinkle onto Jenny's back as she stared into the distance of South Carolina.

Another time, years later, maybe in 2001, I traveled to North Carolina to visit Laura and we drove to South Of The Border, smoking pot the whole way, and super stoned we ran around S.O.B. until dark. It was Thanksgiving. And, in our stoned daze, we played well past dinner and when we came to our senses and drove to her grandmother's house, we pulled out the leftovers from the refrigerator and ate our meal cold.

For those of you who haven't been to South Of The Border, or at least driven past it and the dozens of billboard advertisements along I-95 from Virginia to Georgia, well, then... you're missing out. And I suggest you make a concerted effort to find out for yourself what exactly is South Of The Border. And then let me know. I still have no fuckin' clue as to what that truck-stop, tourist-trap, pay-toilet, cheap fireworks, giant dinosaurs, bigger Mexicans, the biggest sombrero, ice cream parlor, wax museum, I don't know what all that shit is except to say that it's the one, the only South Of The Border.

Camp Close By ran a shuttle, what they called "The Party Bus," to and from the venue both before and after the show. But they only ran it twice, which meant if you missed the first one, it didn't matter. That afternoon I missed the first bus and when I made it back to our tent the zipper was closed and the cooler was closed too. Tim had left without me.

And that was fine.

I stashed the wad of cash in my dirty socks at the foot of my sleeping bag, rolled a joint, grabbed a few eights to sell in the lot, and was off to wait for the second bus. At the bus stop a man sold veggie burritos and balloons full of nitrous. I bought the latter.

When the bus made the bend everyone waiting roared with approval and last minute beer-runs happened. Almost as many hippies ran to the bus as ran away from the bus and then a second wave of smiling, beer-holding hippies arrived.

I hadn't been on a school bus since high school, since North Carolina, and that certainly wasn't "The Party Bus."

Our Party Bus driver got on the speaker and said, "Listen up!"

She was a three-hundred pound black woman. "My name is Monica. And today is my birthday!"

"HAPPY BIRTHDAY MONICA!" sang the hippies.

"So ya'll be good and I'll be good. I don't care what you do or what you got but ya'll need to stay in your seats, alright?"

"Happy birthday!"

"Alright," Monica said. "And if you got any of that weed, go on and pass some up here!"

Everyone howled and someone in the front lit a joint.

The guy next to me was passed out holding three cans of Budweiser still attached in the six-pack plastic ringing. Careful to keep pinching the end of my half-full balloon with one hand, I fingered the plastic ring off a beer can with the other.

POP!

My balloon popped in my hand and someone behind me leaned forward and said, "Oh, man, sorry, I think I popped your balloon with my cigarette."

"Don't worry," I said, opening my beer can.

"Hey, tell Monica to stop the bus!" someone yelled.

I couldn't see him, but apparently there was a man running alongside us waving, desperately trying to get someone to stop the bus.

"Monica, let him on!"

"Let him on!"

"Alright, alright," said Monica, braking, stopping, opening the door.

Juice stepped on board. Shirtless, and wearing a long purple cape, with long surfer hair, he thanked the bus driver and took a seat in the front while everyone applauded.

"Juice!" I called out, but he didn't hear me. "Juice!"

Then Monica blasted the radio and everyone cheered.

I first met Juice in Colorado, hitchhiking from Boulder to Red Rocks for a Trey Anastasio Band concert. At breakfast, I ran into a pair of hippies and asked them if they were heading to the concert at Red Rocks.

"No," says one. "But he was wanting to go. He's visiting from Maine."

"Well, I'm going, but I don't have a ride and I think we should all go together."

"But I don't have a ticket."

"You'll be able to find one down there," I say. "I'll help you."

He thinks about it for a moment.

"I'll drive you if you want to go," his friend says.

So the three of us pile in his car later that afternoon and the driver says, "I just have to make a few stops first."

We go to the bank, the post office, Burger King, his girlfriend's office to deliver the Burger King, then we stop at the drug dealer's house but he isn't home so we go to another drug dealer's house. Then we go back to the bank.

"Don't worry," the driver says. "We're on our way now."

Suddenly the car fills with smoke. We stop and jump out. The driver opens the hood, sees the fire, runs to the trunk where he keeps a jug of water, runs back to the front and douses the fire.

As the last of the smoke clears, the three of us stand dumbfounded.

"Sorry, boys," I say. "I'll see you later."

I walk two blocks to a main intersection, pull my notebook from my backpack, write RED ROCKS on a piece of paper, and hold it up for the passing traffic. Instantly, a topless Jeep Wrangler squeals to a stop.

The passenger is a beautiful, hippie chick in a white dress wearing her long blonde hair in pigtails. The driver is a shirtless man with long blonde hair held down by a headband.

"Hop in, dude," says the driver.

"Thanks," I say, hopping in. "I'm Andy."

"You can call me Juice, little brother."

By the time Juice, his girlfriend, Rose, and I rolled into the lot we were friends. And the first thing Juice did when he stepped out of the Jeep was open his pack and remove a long, purple cape with silver glitter lettering across the shoulders that read *JUICE*.

"I'm ready now, little brother," he said to me. "Let's go for a walk."

In the lot we met up with another carload of their friends and we all took shots and drank beer and smoked opium before I felt that it was time to part.

Wandering around I employed myself with the Orgasmatron for a while but when I ran into some friends from an earlier Colorado concert I put it away and focused on drinking, needing to catch up to their level of intoxication. By the time they were ready to go in, I had only just started and that's where we split up.

I wandered through the lot drinking and making friends and then stumbled upon a table of free Everclear jell-o shots.

"Have a free shot, before they melt," says the girl.

"Everclear?" I ask, already drunk.

"It sure is!" she says. "Come get your free jell-o shots!"

"I'll have one," I say and down it. "Ya know, I haven't done Everclear since junior year of high school when my friend Sparky and I would take pulls of his brother's bottle after school."

"Then you should really have another," someone whispers to me before taking his free shot.

"I should," I say, and take another. "Sparky and I would be drunk through dinner off this shit."

I take another.

"That's all," I say, and move on.

What could only have been an hour later I was beginning to have trouble walking and this guy catches me at some point, rights me up and asks if I want any acid.

"No," I say. "I don't have the money for that today, thank you."

"No, for free," he says.

I cock my head back and look at him down my nose.

He nods.

"Well, sure then," I say. "Why not?"

He takes me to his car where he sits behind the wheel and I sit shotgun and he says, "put your head back and stick out your tongue."

I comply, feel the liquid land on my tongue, close my mouth, open my eyes, and look at him.

He's staring at me. And he looks horrified.

"What?" I ask.

"You've tripped before, right?" he asks.

"Yeah…"

"Good," he says, laughing, patting me on the shoulder. "Because I just gave you like twenty or thirty hits, I don't know, it just poured right out."

He's still laughing as he steps out of the car, leaving me inside to prepare for what would surely be the most intense drug experience of my life.

The very first time I did acid was in my bedroom by myself after buying some tabs at a Phish concert the night before. That was September 1999, I went to the show with my friend Laura and bought acid but she didn't want to trip at the concert so we saved them for the next night but she didn't want to trip then either so I ate them both.

Wrapped in my comforter, squirming around on the floor, I talked with my Bob Dylan poster and at some point during the night I returned to the womb and not long after that I was reborn.

I've done acid a few times in my life, more than a handful, possibly more than two handfuls, but really not that much, relatively speaking. I have friends who have tripped hundreds of times.

But acid can be tricky. I like to stay away from it. You just never really know what it'll do or more importantly, what's in it.

I prefer mushrooms. The trips are always cleaner, without the psychedelic hangover. Although there have been times when I've tripped on mushrooms and just about lost my mind.

One such time was at Mike Force's gallery show at Pratt where Mike and I bought enough mushrooms for not only ourselves but also all our friends. Throughout the opening, friends kept approaching me with leftover mushrooms saying they didn't need any more. And I ate the leftovers every time.

Time was no longer linear in my mind. Time became a sphere, with the present moment at the center and a million possible courses of action shooting out from that center into every direction of an infinite sphere. And the present moment was constantly changing. Every second I was presented with an understanding of millions of simple actions, so many that at times I was paralyzed by the limitless options. At other times, other seconds, it was all I could do to randomly pick a course of action and follow it through. Some of these actions were simple and mundane like putting my hands in my pockets, pulling out my hands from my pockets, that sort, but at some point in the evening I chose the "break a glass" course of action. Then I chose the "kick in the window" course of action. And I began to fear I would harm myself.

Another such intense trip, but still not The Most Intense Drug Experience Of My Life, occurred in Boulder, Colorado. Again, the night before I had bought mushrooms at a Phil and Friends show in Red Rocks, ate half at the show, had an amazing time, and then the next day, just bumming around Boulder, I ate the other half.

That afternoon I went walking down Arapahoe to an aquarium that I had read about. I didn't have the brochure but I knew it was on Arapahoe maybe at the corner of 21st or 22nd Street. Well, the mushrooms grabbed hold of me around 16th or 17th Street. I was seeing characters from *Planet of the Apes* in the clouds. And they were talking to me. And I could hear them.

At some point, maybe 25th Street, I popped in Futon World and asked the proprietor if there was an aquarium in the area. He politely said, no, so I left, but writing this now I can rightfully assume it went more like this:

AP SMITH: "Where's the God-damn aquarium, I know it's around here somewhere!"
FUTON WORLD PROPRIETOR: "Son, you need to leave right now."

I never found that aquarium and whether or not it ever really existed is up for discussion.

Walking around in the heat that afternoon, after my attempt to ask for directions, I felt a little light-headed, tired, hot, so I did the only thing that made sense: I looked for shade.

There, an oasis outside the Safeway grocery store. I reached the shade near the automatic door entrance and loitered between the newspaper bins and the public telephones. Everyone kept coming and going, mothers stared at me and they knew I was tripping, and Charlton Hesston was trying to get my attention.

"I just need to talk to someone," I told myself. "That's all I need."

I riffled through my address book, not thinking about the fact that I'd been tromping around Boulder by myself for weeks now. Sam, I thought. I'll call Sam. She'll make it all better.

I didn't even need her to talk me down. Just having a conversation with her was enough to calm me. But I wanted to sit down and the phone cord wouldn't reach my ear if I sat on the sidewalk but it seemed to be long enough if I sat on top of the phone stand. I put Sam on hold and climbed up top, dangling my feet over the front of the number touch pad.

"What's the matter with you?" Sam asked.

"Nothing," I said. "I just want to rest my feet for a second."

I watched the sidewalk turn into millions of tiny hexagonal puzzle pieces. The tiles started vibrating and bouncing, sometimes rhythmically.

Now I'm floating on my back in the ocean. The sky is fiery red. But the ocean... it's not water. It's turtles. I grab a turtle and hold it in front of my face and watch its little arms and legs punch and kick and then the turtle turns into a rock. Then I grab another turtle and watch him turn into a rock. Then slowly all the turtles I'm floating on turn into rocks and the sky turns blue and I realize I'm lying on my back on a pile of rocks on the ground behind the pubic telephone.

I had fallen off backwards.

How long was I out for?

The phone cord was dead still, the phone hanging motionless. I grabbed it, "Hello," I said.

"Yeah," Sam said. "What happened?"

"How long was I gone for?" I asked.

"A minute or two."

"I have to go, I'll call you back," I said and hung up.

My instinct told me to go into the grocery store and upon entry, when the air conditioning hit me, I realized I was soaking wet as if I'd just jumped in a pool with all my clothes on.

Still tripping in the grocery store I quickly bought a bag of chips and a bottle of water.

"Are you okay?" asked the check out clerk.

"I'm fine," I said, struggling to remember the process for buying an item at a grocery store. Price, money, change, item, thank you.

I'm back outside but still not well. I see a bagel shop across the street and I bound over there. Inside I toss some change on the counter and tell the boy I don't want anything, I just want to rest for a minute.

"Sure thing, dude," he says.

"Thanks," I say and turn to sit but he stops me.

THE LAST AMERICAN GYPSY

"Just go like this," he says, touching the side of his head.

I touch the side of my head and pull my hand away and see that my hand is now covered in blood.

In the bathroom I discover that I'm bleeding from my head, two spots on my back, both knees, and my left arm. Maybe I didn't pass out. Maybe I had a seizure. I was still tripping. And to be cleaning your own blood while tripping is quite a curious experience. But not the most intense.

I was tripping balls before I even got out of the dude's car. Or so I thought, I was wasted drunk too, but if the acid didn't kickn in there then it started on my walk into the venue because when I got to the gates a man handed me giant watermelon and said to share it with my friends. So me and this other dude cracked it open on a rock and then split it again and again until we had small enough pieces to distribute through the crowd of hippies entering the concert. We had our share too.

Inside, I walked past the merchandise table and noticed a T-shirt for sale. And by this point I was definitely tripping. The T-shirt, bright lime green, had on its chest only a small, centered illustration of a wedge of watermelon. I bought that shirt that day. And I still wear it sometimes.

I made my way through the crowd to a seat on the tiered stone surrounded by these massive walls of red rock and there were even a few people picnicking on top. I didn't really know what the hell was going on but when the music started, I began dancing and I didn't stop until the music stopped and then everything was quiet and dark and I was surrounded by people who I thought may or may not want to kill me. Then this pregnant woman walked by and she let me touch her belly and I could see the syrupy light of her unborn child stick to my hand when I pulled it back and forth from her stomach. Then the music started again and I danced some more and found myself talking with this girl who seemed to be rolling pretty hard. She keep clenching her jaw and grinding her teeth and when the music ended again she asked me if that was the end of the second set or the encore.

"I don't know," I said.

I tuned to the guy next to me and asked him if that was the end of the second set or the end of the encore.

"The second set," he said.

"The second set," I told the girl... she was gone. I looked around and I didn't see her anywhere.

To this day I don't know if she ever really existed.

Then after the encore and the house lights came on I knew the concert was over so I followed the crowd out of the venue and up this hill overlooking the parking lot. I had hitched to the show and I still needed a ride back to Boulder so I pulled out my notebook and wrote BOULDER on a piece of paper. I had a lot of fun writing BOULDER, took my time, made the letters bubbly and beautiful and, finished, proud of my work, I looked up and saw that no one else was walking out of the venue. Looking down at the parking lot, I saw that most of the cars and vans were gone.

I started to panic and ran around asking strangers for a ride to Boulder. But no one was heading that way, or so they said.

Finally, a muscular man grabbed me and said, "We're going to Boulder, come with me."

I followed and he led me to a van around which stood a half-dozen CU fraternity brothers. And they were all severely drunk. And slightly mutated, three eyes or extended jaws, large foreheads, and one of them didn't have a nose.

I climbed in the van with them and listened to the passenger argue with the driver as we pulled out of the lot.

"You're way drunker than I am," slurred the passenger.

"No way," slurred the driver.

The van rode the edge of the cliffs of Red Rocks as the brothers slurred and argued and completely ignored me. And the driver rarely looked at the road. I wondered if this serpent seatbelt would save me when we crashed. And if this is how it all ends, then so be it. I was prepared to die. I accepted death and waited for its arrival all the way back to Boulder where we suddenly stopped and I was once again alone in a stranger's vehicle. I stepped out. The frat boys were nowhere in sight. I was in the parking lot of a strip club.

I just started walking.

Soon enough, I came across the bagel shop I sought refuge in the week earlier and it felt nice to see a familiar sight. I had only two more miles to walk to the hostel.

It was well past midnight, maybe even two or later, and no one was on the road. I walked alone and after a mile I grew accustomed to the isolation and began to imagine what houses had unlocked front doors.

Then I came across a fat man sitting at a bus stop but I knew better than to assume he was real. His fat was dripping off him through the cracks in the bench and collecting in a puddle underneath him. He wore a red baseball cap and held a cigar in his hand. The radio on the bench was silent.

I walked past him without making eye contact.

"Be careful out there!" he yelped after me.

"Thanks," I said, somewhat startled.

"No, I mean it, be careful out there!"

"I will, thanks."

"I'm telling you to be careful!" he said. "The aliens are stealing gallons of sperm nightly, I just heard the President say so. Here, listen."

He turned on the radio: *"President Bush today announced that aliens are stealing gallons of..."*

I kept walking.

"Want any acid?" someone asked me on "The Party Bus" on our way to the venue.

"No, thanks," I said, as the bus pulled into the parking lot.

We had arrived and I opened the back emergency door to the bus and all the hippies filed out of the bus from both ends.

I assumed Juice took off running because I couldn't find him in the crowd.

Indiana, I thought.

Then I went through the lot, down parking aisles towards Shakedown. I didn't see Tim or anyone I knew for that matter so I started asking if anyone wanted some pot. Soon enough this little fourteen year old girl and her even younger boyfriend approached me and asked if she could buy some weed for forty dollars.

"Sure," I said, handing her a baggie.

They scrutinized the bag for long enough and then I said, "Okay, that's enough."

"We'll buy it," the girl said, digging into her purse.

"Good," I said.

"Hey, buddy," someone passing said to me.

"Hey," I said.

He leaned in close and whispered, "This is a warning, I don't want to see you doing this again."

While he leaned back, he held his coat open to reveal not only a badge but also a gun. Then he stepped back into the crowd and was gone.

"We only have thirty dollars," the teenie-bopper said.

"Forget it," I said, walking away.

"Okay, forty," she called out.

It wasn't long until I saw Tim and Kevin but before that I ran into Brian and Bubba in passing.

"I was beginning to wonder if you dropped off," Brian said. "I haven't seen you since the Brooklyn shows."

"No, I've been here," I said.

"Are you heading in?"

"Yeah, I think so," I said, thinking of the cop.

"Where you sitting tonight?"

"Where-ever," I said.

"Well, we'll be Page-side, come find us at set break," Brian said.

I entered the gates.

I meandered around the food tents and the beer garden looking for Tim but I didn't see him. So I hit the Porta-Potties.

The line was ridiculous and I started chatting it up with my neighbors, in different lines for different Porta-Potties.

"Wanna bet my line moves quicker than your line?" I asked one.

"Uh..." the guy said, craning his neck to count the number of women in his line versus the number of women in my line. My line had fewer women. "No, I don't want to bet," he said.

But in all my years of gambling on Porta-Potty lines, the women rarely make much of a difference. Looking at any drunk or drinking man, can you tell me if he's going to piss for thirty seconds or for three and a half minutes?

"You wanna bet?" I asked another neighbor

"How much?" he said.

"Five bucks?" I said.

"Five bucks won't even buy me a beer," he said. "How about ten?"

"Yeah, okay," I said.

"You got ten bucks?"

"Yeah, I got ten bucks, show me yours."

So we each waited on line with ten-dollar bills in our hands and sure enough my turn came first and when the door opened and the girl stepped out and I stepped in I heard all our in-line neighbors roar. I pissed, stepped out, held the door for the next guy, collected my winnings, and was on my way down the line when I came across a girl heading the other direction carrying two beers.

"Can I have one of those?" I asked.

"Uh," she said, stopping. "I guess."

She handed me a beer and kept walking.

"Is that your girlfriend?" asked the next on line.

"No," I said, drinking.

"How do you know her?"

"I don't," I said.

"Well, fuck..." he said. "Then give me a sip!"

I handed him the beer and we laughed as he drank.

"Andy!" someone said.

I looked around.

"Andy!"

It was Tim, about three Porta-Potty lines down.

The show that night was damn good. I danced my ass off. And I spent some of my new money on beers for Tim and me.

After the show, Tim rushed us out to the bus because someone told him "they give out spaghetti when you get back, but only if you're on the first bus."

This sounded fantastic to me. I was drunk and, as Tim later told me, I made a fool out of myself at the bus stop shouting generally misogynistic remarks at passing girls.

But we got on the first bus.

But Monica wasn't our bus driver.

It was Debra. And it was her birthday too.

Back at Camp Close By we debarked and sure enough, there was an assembly line of cooks and servers waiting for us. Not only did Tim and I each receive a heaping bowl of spaghetti and sauce, but the last server in the line gently laid one, single vegetarian meat ball on top.

Tim and I ate as we walked and were finished by the time we reached our camp and lit a joint. That night we each fell asleep early. But I woke up in the middle of the night because our neighbors were playing charades or some other kind of guessing game.

I climbed out of the tent, opened a beer and sat to smoke a cigarette.

This guy in passing asked me for a light so I gave him one and then he asked me if I wanted to smoke a bowl so I said yes and then he sat down.

"Devin," he said, holding out his hand.

"Andy," I said, and shook his hand.

We smoked and talked about the show and the free spaghetti–he was on the second bus and missed it–and then towards the end of it he asked me if I wanted a balloon.

"Sure," I said.

"Be right back," he said and ran off.

He was back almost immediately with two balloons and we huffed them quickly.

WAWAWAAAWAAWAWAWAAA

"You know," he said, in a deep voice. "I know where we could buy a tank right here at this camp."

"A tank?" I asked, with surprisingly deep voice.

"Yeah, a tank, you interested?"

"A little," I said.

"Well, come with me, I'll show you."

So I followed Devin towards the entrance of the campsite, really the dividing line between the parking area and the camping area. Guarding this border was a stocky, short guy on a four-wheeler. His shirt read, Camp Close By.

"Hey buddy," said Devin to the camp employee.

"What's up?" he said.

"My buddy and I wanted to take you up on that offer," Devin said.

"The two of you?"

"Yeah."

"I don't think I can take both of you on my four-wheeler," said the employee.

"Sure, you can," said Devin. "I'll ride here on the front and he'll ride on back."

"Alright," said the employee. "Hop on."

I held on to the stocky man as he drove us through camp, around the pond, and down a small trail in a corn field to a large, once-red, now black and brown barn. He stopped the four-wheeler about twenty feet from the barn and told us to "wait here."

He walked around the barn and out of sight.

I looked at Devin. He was grinning madly.

The front doors to the barn opened and a man stood in the doorway motioning for us. Devin leading, we walked to the barn, stepped in, and the man closed the doors behind us.

The bar walls, on both floors, were lined, some three and four deep, with hundreds of sixty-pound tanks full of nitrous-oxide gas.

"How many you'd wanted?" asked the doorman. He looked like James Spader. Only older. And slightly cross-eyed.

"How many did we want?" Devin asked me.

"How much are they?" I asked.

"Three hundred," said the doorman.

I didn't really want to buy one in the first place.

"How much do you have?" I asked Devin.

"No, this is all you," he said. "All you."

The doorman waited for me to say something.

I said, "I don't have three hundred dollars."

"Don't waste my time," said the doorman. "Get the fuck outta here."

We walked out and saw the four-wheeler driver on his mount. Our ride was waiting for us. But he looked confused.

The doorman for the driver to leave.

"Assholes," said the driver, gunning off into the cornfield.

"I trust you remember the way back," said the doorman as he closed the barn doors.

"Let's go," said Devin.

"Fuck you," I said. "Three hundred dollars?"

"Whatever, dude, let's go."

We walked into the cornfield and a few yards deep Devin stopped and yelped, "Wasn't that ridiculous!"

"What?"

"That was insane, don't you realize? I didn't care if you bought a tank or not I just wanted to see if it was true! Holy shit, man!" Devin started laughing.

I laughed too.

"Oh, man, that shit was just too much," Devin said, and continued walking.

A.P. SMITH

PART FOUR

At Some Time Or Another, We're All Miracle-Seekers

In 2002 I flew to Virginia for a few Phish concerts. In the winter of 2003 I drove through New England, then flew to North Carolina for a series of Phish concerts. That same summer I flew to Washington for a pair of concerts, and on my way back to New York I scheduled a layover in Kansas City for a Phish concert. Back in New York I drove down to North Carolina then back up through West Virginia to New Jersey for a few more concerts. Then I flew to Miami for the 2003 New Year's run. And this last summer I drove first from Brooklyn to Wisconsin and then a month later back down to Virginia for a concert, then up to Boston for a pair, then continued north to Vermont for Phish's final festival.

    Not counting any transportation time or road time or hotel time, only time spent in the parking lot before the show or inside the venue itself, I've spent over eleven days of my life at Phish concerts.

THE LAST AMERICAN GYPSY

And of the twelve shows I saw during the summer of 2004, I arrived at only one with a ticket. Of the eight shows I saw during the summer of 2003, I arrived to only four shows with tickets. And each afternoon I arrived without a ticket was an afternoon I spent separated from my friends, comfortable with their tickets in their back pockets. While they drank and celebrated, I more often wandered through the parking lot with a finger in the air, hoping someone would be kind enough to sell me his extra ticket.

Some shows were easier to get than others. In Miami for New Years, people couldn't give away their extra tickets. There were tickets covering the sidewalk in front of the gates to the venue. On the other hand, at the first Brooklyn show last summer, no one had extra tickets. It was the tour's kick off show and the band was playing at Coney Island. It was raining and the lot was full of wet miracle-seekers, myself included. That afternoon I ended up paying the subway fare and cutting all the miracle-seekers at the turnstiles so I could hit the incoming pedestrians first. Eventually, I bought a ticket for just under face but it wasn't for trying, and standing in the rain, and desperately running into the train station, and cutting ahead of a dozen other ticket-less hippies.

It was a similar experience finding a ticket for the second night at Coney Island. No, that's just not right. I remember now. Brian sold me that ticket. And that was the night Jay-Z joined Phish on stage for a couple of songs, including "99 Problems."

In Burgettstown two summers back Tim bought four tickets off a guy for a hundred dollars flat so he gave me one, took one for himself, and sold the other two for fifty apiece.

And at The Gorge that summer I bought a ticket for ten bucks.

But this last summer, it wasn't that easy. I paid seventy dollars for a fifty dollar ticket in Saratoga. Sixty in Virginia. Seventy for the first night in Mansfield, Mass. And seventy for the second night in Indiana.

But it was that second night in Mansfield that really worried me.

We got to the lot real late, maybe only two hours before show time and Tim had his ticket already so I was on my own. I ran around from friend to friend, asking all of them if they knew of anyone and when they each said no I asked for them to keep their ears open.

Walking along the entrance with my finger in the air, I counted over twenty other miracle-seekers. We were everywhere.

Almost as many people had their fingers up as didn't.

Someone was singing, "Birds of a feather... Are flocking outside..."

"This looks pretty grim," I told a girl with her finger in the air.

"I know," she said, genuinely concerned. "I've never been shut out of a show," she said.

"Me neither," I said.

"Tonight might be that night," she said.

I couldn't accept that. "Good luck," I said.

"You too," she said. "And if you can't find one we're all gonna rush just after the second song."

I made my way back through the lot and around again but most everyone was inside the venue by this time. A steady stream of cars still poured into the lot but all the miracle-seekers lined both sides of those cars from entrance to aisle.

I walked back to Tim's car and grabbed a few packs of cigarettes. I had given up and figured I should at least work if I'm not going to get in the show.

I hit the gates and stood with my back to the entrance holding up in one hand a pack of Camel Lights and a pack of Marlboro Lights. I held my beer in the other hand. I sold a few packs instantly and then just as quickly a pair of police officers approached me, took my packs and my beer and handcuffed me.

I didn't ask any questions and they didn't say a word and after about ten minutes they unlocked my cuffs and sent me on my way.

I stepped into a rather densely foliaged area and took a piss, thinking I shouldn't give up and that I've never been shut out but the show's about to start and it doesn't look good so maybe tonight was the night I stayed in the parking lot. Zipping my fly, I accepted that.

But coming out of the bushes I stuck my finger in the air anyway and I held up my last pack of cigarettes too. Making my way across the stream of incoming traffic, a driver called out to me. "Cigarettes," he said.

I walked up to his window. "Five bucks," I said and handed him the pack.

"How's this?" he asked, handing me a ticket.

"Even better," I said. Then I screamed. "Thank you, thank you, thank you," I said.

"No problem," he said. "I've been in your position. Thanks for the smokes."

The last time I was in Massachusetts was on the roadtrip during the Democratic National Convention and the time before that was for Phish's Twentieth Anniversary Show and the time before that was for the Worcester show on Winter Tour 2003.

Again, it was Sam and me in Worcester. We took a bus up to Boston where we stayed at a hotel and then took a train to Worcester and shared a cab to the venue. The morning after the show we wandered around Boston and eventually landed at a historical landmark turned mini-mall where we stopped at Ben and Jerry's and the employee, a red-haired Santa Claus who called himself Rainbow, served us ice cream and then asked me if I caught the show in Worcester.

"I did," I said.

"How was it?" he asked.

"Pretty good," I said.

"I wanted to go but..."

"Next time," I said.

"Hey, have you ever tried salvia?"

"Tried what?"

"It's a lot like pot but it's totally legal and it gives you this crazy high," Rainbow told me.

"Okay."

"Wanna try some?" he asked. "I'll roll you a joint right now."

I watched Rainbow pull out of his pocket a bag of what looked like pot. And he started to roll a joint right there on the counter.

"What are you doing?" asked Sam.

"Nothing," I said.

Rainbow handed me this joint of salvia. "Now go outside and smoke this and come back and tell me what you think," said Rainbow.

"Okay," I said, taking the joint. "Sam, let's go."

Outside the mall I lit the joint and started smoking.

"Sam?" I offered.

"No thanks," she said. "I don't smoke weird shit from people named Rainbow before noon."

So I smoked the whole thing myself, waited a minute, and still felt nothing.

"Let's go back in," I said.

Walking in the mall back towards the Ben and Jerry's I didn't feel even the slightest bit high. Then it hit me and suddenly I was floating above my body watching myself with a third person perspective as I walked through the mall. Then it was over. We had reached the Ben and Jerry's.

"Well?" Rainbow asked, excitedly.
"It was definitely something," I said.
"That's right," Rainbow replied.

That was in February and in May I was in New Orleans at my grandmother's house late one night watching television with my father. We were stoned. Channel-surfing, we landed on Comedy Central's *Insomniac*. And Dave Attell, the show's host, was in Boston being chased by a red-headed, overall-clad Santa Claus.

"What you say your name was?" Dave Attell asked, while retreating.
"Rainbow," he said.
"Jesus, dad," I said. "I know that guy."
"Which one?" my father asked.
"Rainbow," I said. "He gave me this weird shit to smoke when I was in Boston last winter."
"What was it?" my father asked.
"It was *something*," I said.

I think that's what I'll tell my children when they ask me about Phish tour. When I'm old and whittling and I hear my teenage son blasting Phish on his stereo, I'll stomp in there and whoop his ass.

But really, if I have children, and they indeed ask me about the experiences I had while following the band Phish, I'll tell them it was something. "It was something," I'll say. "Some of the best times of my life," I'll say. "That was when I was younger, older than you, but still a kid. And I don't know about The Grateful Dead, and I only know a little about Phish, but I can honestly say this: it was all about the music."

"You didn't do drugs, dad?"

"Of course, I did drugs," I'll say. "But that's not why I went to Phish shows. I went for the music. For that moment when you're dancing with your eyes closed and the world disappears."

"Shut up, dad."

"No, I'm serious. Maybe you'll have one of those moments in your life, maybe you already have. And if you have, you understand. Maybe you'll have dozens, even hundreds of those moments. I know I have. Music is special in that way. And Phish was special to me because of that."

"Whatever, dad."

"*Whatever*," I'll mock.

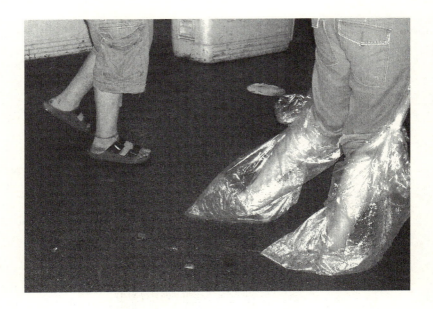

PART FIVE

The Final Drive, The Final Festival, The Final Concert:
Coventry, Vermont

I woke up in my tent alone. What sounded like the roar of a beastly car engine just rampaged past my tent. Outside familiar music was playing but what woke me was not the nearby and distant ambient noise of a dozen boom boxes playing Phish or Moe or String Cheese Incident or Disco Biscuits. No, what woke me up that first morning at Coventry was the roar of a beastly car engine rampaging past my tent.

In my sleepy stupor, I heard cheers and applause.

"Is someone in that tent?" I heard a girl ask.

In my tent with me I had my pack, a few cartons of cigarettes, and my sleeping bag, which I collapsed upon late last night. The blue vinyl walls of my tent are glowing from the high noon sun. I assumed it was around noon.

Still dressed from last night, I unzipped my door and poured myself out into the world. The sun was bright and the air smelled fresh but still cool and damp, definitely before noon.

Tim and those camping with us or near us, including his girlfriend and her brother, cheered and exclaimed, "He's alive!"

"Morning," I said, stretching, reaching to the sky. I yawned, roaring.

"Dude," Tim said. "You almost died." He points to the other side of my tent where I see deep tire tracks in the mud heading first for higher ground then swerving right, heading straight for my tent, then deep left avoiding my tent by only a few feet.

"They were gunning out the mud and man we all thought you were awake but then they started sliding right for your tent and dude…" said a bright-eyed hippie, laughing. "They almost took you out!"

I laughed, said my good mornings to everyone, made myself a Bloody Mary from the cooler, sat down and surveyed the scene.

We had arrived late last night straight from Mansfield, Massachusetts, skipping the Camden show. We cruised up back roads, mostly state routes I fingered out on the map to avoid traffic, but then, as expected, when we reached Vermont's Route 5, we hit a stand-still. I started drinking rum and coke in the backseat while we listened to the Camden show live on the Coventry Festival radio station, The Bunny.

It's an interesting sensation to be in a line of thousands of cars parked on a road that normally would allocate forty or fifty miles an hour. Along Route 5 there are homes and families, some of whom stood in their front lawns with tables and tents, selling anything from homemade jewelry to hot dogs to smores.

Four or five hours later, nothing terrible really, we rolled onto Airport Road and into the Festival grounds, the Newport State Airport with crisscrossing runways.

We arrived a full two nights before the weekend of concerts so the camping area we were assigned was relatively close to the runways and the main drag of commerce and gathering, an area much too large to call Shakedown Street.

It wasn't raining when we arrived but the ground was wet and a little muddy so as soon as we parked, all the gypsies jumped out of their caravans; everyone scrambled madly to set up camp on the driest patches and make claim to areas large enough for their factions. The scene was quite chaotic and frenzied.

Boyfriends yelled at girlfriends setting up tents without first laying down tarps. Neighbors argued over communal space now deemed individual territory. Some hippies abandoned their caravans all together and carried what they could up the nearby hill to camp on higher ground. I stood there watching the whole scene drinking my drink until Tim yelled at me to set up my tent as to complete the half-circle of our camp.

"Hey, man," a neighbor said to me. "Do you have any D size batteries?"

"No, sorry," I said, continuing to pitch my tent, which, while holding a drink in one hand, wasn't working at all. I decided to rest and relax, finish my drink, before setting up camp.

Tim's girlfriend, Becca, approached me and asked if I was going to set up tonight or, from the looks of it, in the morning.

"I haven't decided yet," I said.

"But what if you meet some cute girl tonight, where will you take her if you don't have a tent?"

"I'll take her back to *her* tent," I said, finishing my drink. Then I thought it over. "Alright, come on, give me a hand with these stakes here."

And we set up my tent together while everyone else, all set up, sat down for their first beers of the night. It was maybe one or two in the morning.

A neighboring gypsy, a long-haired bearded guy with a light complexion, introduced himself and asked if anyone wanted to smoke so we sat around and smoked a joint until the neighbor said he was going to go towards the entrance and grab a bite from one of the vendors over there.

"I'll take a walk," I said. "Let me just freshen my drink."

We got acquainted walking though the aisles of cars and caravans and tents and canopies. His name was Charlie and he was from New Mexico, worked for Southwest Airlines, flew out to Boston for free where he rented a car and drove up to Vermont for the weekend.

"My girlfriend couldn't get off work," he said, as we tromped towards the runway. "She wouldn't like this mud anyway. I don't know what we're gonna do if it turns out like they say it will."

"What do you mean?" I ask.

"Didn't you see the weather? Vermont's expecting like six tropical storms this weekend. This whole place is gonna turn to mud."

We kept walking, trying not to imagine the impending doom of a 100,000 caravans, 100,000 hippies, all huddled together waist-deep in mud.

Walking up the runway against the flow of incoming traffic, I asked those with windows down if they had extra tickets. Some got the joke and laughed while others offered an apologetic, "no."

Amidst the dark landscape of a tangled jungle of campsites and vendors, illuminated somewhat frighteningly by a sparse forest of tall, stadium lights, Charles and I soaked up our new home, where we would live for the next five days and nights. I made note of the tall stadium light closest to our camp for the return voyage.

At the entrance we ordered food from the large tented caravan of some global hippie cult. Their set up was rather sweet: a wooden caravan, with some on-site assembly surely required, complete with a kitchen and seating area. Charlie ordered a gyro and I ordered a slice of apple pie.

Back at the site most of our crew was gone and Charlie and I found Tim sitting drinking with one of the volunteer parking/camping attendants. They were drinking my beer.

Tim had pulled out his boom box and tuned it to The Bunny, which was now playing its rotation of its station call letters: "B-U, B-U, B-U-N-N-Y. B-U, B-U, B-U-N-N-Y."

"How's it look out there?" Tim asked.

"Crowded," I answered, opening a beer.

"Yo," said the volunteer parking attendant. "Can I get another beer?"

"Uh, sure," I said. "What's your name?"

"Oh, sorry," he said, shaking my hand. "I'm Jack. Isn't this great?"

"Yeah," I said.

"Have you guys been doing the whole tour?"

"Yup."

"Wow," he said, gulping his beer. "I've never seen Phish, never been to a Phish concert, but my buddies said we should all volunteer so I came along and I've just been meeting all these nice, amazing people from all over and drinking beer and smoking pot and just... you are just the nicest people in the world, did you know that?"

We laughed and the radio started playing that Fat Boy Slim song that loops Christopher Walken saying, "I've got a fever, and the only prescription is more cowbell."

"More cowbell!" screamed someone in the distance.

Some people screamed with primitive joy.

An explosion of fireworks lit up the campground.

Even more people screamed.

The next morning, after a few Bloody Marys, I went walking on my own through the grounds and the daylight made it that much more apparent: thousands had gathered here for the weekend for Phish's final concert.

Walking along the runway, flanked on both sides by vendors selling food and T-shirts and paraphernalia, I passed teenagers, twenty-somethings, middle-aged women, elderly men, couples with babies, the whole spectrum of gypsy demographics had made their way to Coventry to see this band play two more concerts.

Everyone was smiling, happy to be there and happier to be there a day early because that meant today could be a day to wander freely among the throngs, a day without schedule, a day of preparation for the forty-eight hour party on the horizon.

But some had started partying already, myself included, and we were the ones who had already abandoned our shoes. We held beers in our hands and extra cans in our pockets and walked flat-footed and slow. One such hippie, a cute teenage girl with a crew-cut, was walking alongside me and when I said, "hello," she said:

"Would you like some mushroom chocolates?"

"Yes, yes, I would," I said.

"Okay, great, let's go over here."

We made our way off the runway between vendors and found and dry spot under someone's canopy and took a seat. She showed me the chocolates and I talked her down from thirty to twenty a piece and then bought two.

"Where are you from?" she asked.

"Brooklyn," I said.

"Oh, wow, weren't those Coney Island shows just the best?"

I agreed.

"Yeah, I'm from Wisconsin, making my way across the country with the band."

"That's wonderful," I said.

"Do you want to smoke, are you on your way to someone?"

"No, I'd love to smoke," I said.

"Great," she said, removing a pipe and a bag from her satchel. "I had to make some quick gas money for a friend I owe so I got these chocolates but you just bought the last of them so I think I can take a break for a minute."

"Of course you can," I said, licking my lips. This girl couldn't be older than sixteen, I thought.

"How long have you been growing your dreads?" she asked.

"Almost four years," I said.

She reached out and gave one a squeeze. "That's wonderful," she said, then rubbed her head. "I had to cut mine off at the beginning of tour."

"That's too bad."

"Yeah," she said. "Bugs."

"Bugs?"

She lit the bowl and inhaled and then, exhaling and cloud of smoke, she said, "Lice."

I hit the bowl myself. "Bummer," I said, exhaling.

She nodded.

I nodded.

Someone walked past us with a glance and a smile.

"I love traveling," she said. "It's really the only time I feel free, free to wander, free to see new things, free to meet new people..." she motioned to me.

I hit the bowl again, nodding.

"But I miss home, miss my friends, I miss my iguana," she said.

"What's his name?" I asked.

"Her," she said, hitting the bowl. "Her name is Pandora."

"I used to have an iguana," I said.

"Really? What happened?"

"He ran away," I said.

"That's so sad," she said, looking at me sorrowfully. Then her look changed.

I leaned in slowly and kissed her small lips. She kissed back, scooting closer and we held each other kissing sweetly, without tongue.

Then she pulled away and giggled, blushing, and I chuckled, and kissed her again, running my hand along the back of her neck up her peach fuzz head.

I heard someone walking up but I didn't hear them walk past so I pulled away and saw a guy digging in the cooler near the van under the canopy we were sitting under.

He sat down in a chair with a beer and smiled at us.

The girl packed up her bowl and her pot and smiled, saying, "I should go, I'll see you later." Then she gave me a kiss and trotted off through nearby cars.

"Sorry, dude," the sitting hippie said. "Want a beer?"

"Sure," I said.

He gave me a beer, I thanked him, and made my way back to the runway, which I walked along until reaching the familiar blue and gray van that I knew to turn after into the camping and walk straight until finding my camp. Charlie was sitting there smoking a joint so I sat with him and said I got some mushroom chocolates if he wanted one.

"How much?" he asked.

"Thirty," I said.

"Sure," he said, so I traded him hallucinogenic chocolate for cash and we each ate our pieces.

Later that afternoon and into evening, Charlie and I walked along the runway tripping and selling cigarettes to passing gypsies. The competition was tough as most people who were there, hippies who had arrived a day early, were well prepared, meaning they either had a supply of cigarettes or a surplus and were selling right along with me.

Standing barefoot on the runway, I studied the faces of the passing hippies hoping to catch a familiar one but I didn't see a single friend that afternoon. Then suddenly the air grew humid and dark clouds coasted in and almost instantly a fierce pelting of rain hit the campgrounds. Charlie took off running without a word and I followed a pair of girls under one of the Coventry information tents for shelter.

An information volunteer came over and told me, and everyone, we couldn't stand there and that it's just water. I pulled out a pack of cigarettes and handed him two. He put one behind his ear and the other in his mouth and lit it. "You can't smoke here either," he told me, smiling.

The rain continued to fall in sheets. Semi-transparent walls of rain could be seen on the horizon. Rain collected in puddles and I watched those puddles grow and grow and grow until a thin sheet of floodwater coated the ground.

Then the rain stopped and the information tent emptied.

I walked back to the runway crossroads where I stood selling cigarettes until evening when the carton was gone and I had fifty dollars in my pocket. Then I made my way back to camp where I found Tim and Becca and all sitting, scowling, drinking, soaking wet.

"How are you dry?" Tim asked me as I walked up.

"I stayed out of the rain," I said, laughing, sitting. "You have any pot?"

"Are you tripping?"

THE LAST AMERICAN GYPSY

"Maybe," I said, pupils undoubtedly dilated. "Where's Charlie?"

"Haven't seen him all day," Tim said, pulling out his pipe. "Thought he was with you."

"He was," I said, laughing, remembering how quickly he ran when it started raining. I was laughing hysterically. "He *was* with me," I said.

"You're tripping face," Tim said, laughing, handing me the bowl.

"Did you meet any girls? They're everywhere!" Becca said.

"Yeah," I said, hitting the pipe. "Yeah, I made a friend."

The gypsy identity is often considered or described as the "other," as the gypsies represent an alternative to social norms and conventions. Now because of this majority-held view of gypsies, methods of control and dispatch can be seen in the gypsy encampments and congregations, meaning, the majority of society controls the gypsies by keeping them on the outskirts, pooled together under certain regional and timely restraints be those festivals or otherwise.

Coventry was to be the last great gathering of the American gypsies, and unbridled revelry would be the theme of this event. Quite bluntly, no one cared how or under what conditions we were all allowed to be at the Newport State Airport that weekend. We just knew this would be the last time. All bets were off. Anything could happen. And the familiar underlying commerce of tour was trumped by the communal feeling of a Louisiana jazz band funeral procession.

We had come to Vermont for the death of this band but we would not mourn. We would celebrate and dance and see this event for what it truly was: one last ride, one last song, one last party.

The end had been coming, even before the band's two-year hiatus from 2000-2002. Then, after hiatus ended, everyone was happy and joyous for the return of this culture and lifestyle, for without jam bands, specifically Phish, all these gypsies are homeless, or, more correctly, bound to their homes. And in gypsy culture, if that's not "homelessness," it's at least imprisonment.

Because after this, it's all over.

The afternoon of the first pair of concerts I woke slowly, sipping my Bloody Mary through a straw. I had tripped all afternoon and then again from midnight to dawn and the next afternoon, rainy and wet, was a perfect fit for my disposition. I stayed close to camp that afternoon, just resting up for what would surely be a long, eventful evening.

The campgrounds, relatively speaking, were calm and quiet, but a long line of caravans still consistently poured in through the gates.

Meanwhile, The Bunny, periodically announced an utter lack of campgrounds as the rain had muddied the airport, rendering it uninhabitable. The festival organizers were in a panic, parking cars and buses on the runways, in surrounding farmland, anywhere they could and the radio claimed tens of thousands of gypsy hippies still clogged Route 5 even then, mere hours from show time.

"I have a fever, and the only prescription is more cowbell."

Someone screamed.

I called my parents.

"I hear it's kinda muddy up there," my dad says. "It made the national news last night. Traffic looks terrible."

"Yeah, I guess they're lined up for miles and miles," I say. "That's why we got here early."

"So is it muddy?"

"Yup," I say, standing ankle-deep in cold, thick muck. A hippie trudging past me squeals as he slips and falls into the mud.

"What was that?" my dad asks.

"Some dude," I say.

"Andy!" Tim yells. "Come here."

"I gotta go, dad. Just wanted to give a call and say I'm here."

"Alright, have fun."

I find Tim smoking pot and he says, "The radio just said they're giving full refunds for tickets because they just can't park any more cars. They're turning people away!"

"Holy shit!"

"Yeah," Tim says, handing me the joint. "Turning them away…"

I sip the joint, thinking. "Turning them away?"

"Turning them away…"

What happened next still amazes me to this day. Of the some 10,000 hippies in their cars parked on Route 5, some having been there for over twenty-four hours, excluding the few hundred that turned back and drove home, all the rest parked their cars, locked their doors, grabbed their gear and walked as much as ten miles into the festival campgrounds. The gypsies abandoned their caravans and walked to the final concert. They poured in by foot in droves by the thousand and set up tents wherever they pleased. It was quite miraculous in that human spirit of determination sort of way.

I was impressed.

Late that afternoon Tim and a few of us headed to the stage where we agreed upon a home-base half-way up the hill on Page-side and I cut the long line into the beer garden where I sat and drank for a good hour before I finally saw a friend I didn't travel with: Dave.

I met Dave somewhere on tour 2003 and caught up with him if not every show then every other show. We had a good time together that summer. He likes to dance as much, if not more, than I do. And Dave is always smiling.

But at Coventry in the beer garden, he looked wrecked. Beaten. Haggard and worse.

"How the fuck are you?" I asked, after we smiled and hugged.

"We just got here," he said.

"What do you mean?" I asked.

"We *just* got here," he said. "My car is parked on Route 5 about seven miles down. We walked in, walked straight here, to the beer garden. I mean, we *just* fucking got here."

"Wow."

"Yeah..."

"But you made it, man, you're here."

"Yeah..."

"It's gonna be worth it," I said.

"We'll see," he said, finishing his beer.

"Sit tight," I said. "Let me go grab us another beer."

"I'll be here," he said, rubbing his forehead.

I waited in line, ordered two beers and the girl handed them to me without asking for money. Then she said, "next," so I walked away.

Back with Dave, his girlfriend was there too, and the three of us chatted a bit about the Mansfield shows and slowly but surely Dave came back to life and by the time I left him and his girl, they were both smiling widely, happy to be there.

Making my way back to Tim and all I heard someone call my name. It was Brian with Bubba and the rest of his crew.

It was quite a reunion and everyone was thrilled to see me.

"Did you guys walk in?" I asked.

"Fuck no," Brian said. "We jumped in the car just before encore at Camden and made it up here around midnight last night."

"Twenty-four hours in the car," Bubba said.

"But it was worth it," Brian said. "Wasn't Camden amazing! YEM into Ghost into Maze into fuckin' Catapult back into Maze!"

"Yeah, I listened to it on The Bunny," I said. "We skipped Camden."

Brian and crew were stunned and silent, almost apologetic.

"Well," Brian said. "That's cool, this is what it's all about anyway."

"Yeah," I said, sorry to disappoint the boys.

"Where you sitting?"

"Half-way up, Page-side."

"Alright, man," Brian said. "We'll see you there, we gotta cruise Mike's side for Tom and Eric."

"See you soon," I said, and we parted.

I found Tim and Charlie and the rest.

"Andy," Charlie called to me. He held a bag of mushrooms in his hand.

"Oh yeah?" I asked.

He nodded.

I dug in the bag and tossed a handful in my mouth. "Thanks, Charlie," I said.

"Sure," he said, eyes wide and pupils dilated. "This shit is really good."

We settled in for the show, which would start within the hour. Everyone around us looked ready, happy, smiling, anxious for the music.

Men comprise the majority of Phish audiences but at Coventry there was a pleasantly surprising amount of women, maybe a 60-40 split unlike the usual 80-20. Some had brought chairs to the stage, some blankets, some just beer or bottled water. As with most any concert, security searched bags and purses at the entrance to the stage area. But as with most Phish concerts, you could get anything inside. I saw people with full cases of beer. I saw a few bongs in the crowd too.

"What do you think?" Tim asked me.

"Hhmmmm..." I said. He was asking me about my pick for an opening song.

Tim and I, throughout the runs we made together, developed quite a knack, as most any tour kid does, for predicting set lists. Honestly, for most any shows we saw together, we could predict, between the two of us, every song Phish played. First it was a game, then a contest, and then more of a science than anything else.

After a long drive between shows it's not uncommon for the band to play Contact.

As an encore for a mediocre show, the band may play Good Times Bad Times.

And at a show with many ticketless people listening outside the venue, the band is likely to play Birds Of A Feather.

For instance, at the third night of New Year's shows in Miami, without Tim, Sam doubted my set list prediction skills, so I wrote down a list of five songs I thought were coming based only on the previous two concerts. And Phish played all five that night. Also, the night before, at that same run in Miami, I sold a pack of cigarettes to a man who looked just like Jim Morrison so I told Sam's brother that Phish would cover a Door's tune. Sure enough they played Break On Through.

"I'm thinking Disease," I told Tim. "Or maybe Twist. Or even 46 Days."

"No way," Tim said. "Maybe 46 Days, but I doubt it."

"Then what?"

"Either YEM or AC/DC Bag," Tim said.

"They won't open with YEM," I said.

"We'll see."

Then the audience howled and everyone sitting stood up. Phish had taken the stage.

The show was spectacular. I danced and sang and everyone in the audience let loose and shed any inhibitions or expectations, specifically the pressures we often put on the band to play certain songs. I've been to shows where fans are outwardly disappointed to hear songs like Friday or Free but at that show, everyone enjoyed the music. And the band played practically flawlessly.

They listened to each other and Trey held back just enough to give the other boys opportunities to lead the band in different directions, directions Trey wouldn't normally take the music.

But most importantly, they enjoyed themselves.

At one point, I closed my eyes for a jam, as I often do, and danced calmly, swaying, letting the music wash over me and everyone else around me. Nothing mattered. I was barely a physical being. The whole mess of reality bottlenecked into a single song, an improvised jam by four talented musicians.

If this comes off as anything but sincere and heartfelt, I apologize. That's a failure on my part as a writer. But if it does feel genuine and unadulterated, let it be known that I've only experienced that moment listening to Phish, and any altered state I may have been in would only have enhanced that sensation and not created it.

The next afternoon I woke wearing the same clothes yet again. In the previous three nights the mud had made its way into my tent, into my sleeping bag, my underwear, my ears, under my fingernails, and dried into a thick cast from my toes to my calves.

I climbed out the tent and stepped into the cold, juicy mud, something of a comfort after sleep.

A light drizzle landed upon my face as I stretched and yawned and I joined Tim, the only one awake, under the canopy.

"Morning," Tim said.

Set list 8/14/04

Set 1
    Walls of the Cave ->
    Runaway Jim ->
    Gotta Jibboo
    You Enjoy Myself ->
    Sample in a Jar
    Axilla
    Poor Heart
    Run Like an Antelope
    Fire

Set 2
    AC/DC Bag ->
    46 Days ->
    Halley's Comet ->
    Ya Mar
    [Trey speech]
    David Bowie
    Character Zero

Set 3
    Twist ->
    The Wedge
    Stash ->
    Free
    [Trey speech]
    Guyute
    Drowned ->
    jam ->
    Friday

Encore
    Harry Hood

"Morning," I said, opening the cooler, remembering I had finished my Bloody Mary mix the previous morning. I opened a beer and sat down.

"I have a fever!" someone screamed.

"More fuckin' cowbell!" someone else screamed.

Tim and I laughed and he lit a joint and I turned on The Bunny.

"This is an important announcement," the DJ spoke. "For those of you who parked your cars on Route 5 yesterday and walked in..."

The campsite howled.

"Just to let you know, your cars won't be towed. So please don't rush out after tonight's concert. Your cars can remain parked until three PM tomorrow, so no procrastinating, but just don't rush out. Again, if you parked your cars..."

"That's a joke," I said, hitting the joint.

"What?" Tim asked.

"As if they even had the capabilities to tow 10,000 cars! Where the fuck would they put them?"

"More cowbell!" someone yelled.

"Yeah, I guess you're right," Tim said, picking at his feet.

I looked at mine. They were rugged, cut and splintered. In an effort to battle the mud, the festival organizers laid down tons of wood chips but almost entirely in vain.

Tim and I spent that morning, rather afternoon, pulling splinters from our feet and smoking pot and listening to The Bunny that replayed last night's Phish concert.

And soon enough, it was time for us to make our way back to the stage.

Waiting for the band, the audience was calmer than usual, generally slow moving. After settling in, Page-side once again, I went meandering through the crowd in search of a few friends I had yet to see. I feared they were of the few who turned back. But then again, there were thousands of hippies at Coventry that weekend and the likelihood of me seeing all of my friends, even though it was extremely likely at each show on tour, the likelihood of seeing them at this Festival was slim to none. Or so that's how I justified it.

The audience seemed tired and somber and especially muddy. Everyone wore looks of exhaustion or so it seemed to me. They could have merely been thinking too hard. This was the final concert. And for some of these people, some of these gypsies, this meant a lot more than that. It meant a lifestyle, or at least a community, was dying. And some, unless I imagined it, seemed to blame the band for all of this.

On the other hand, I respect Phish's decision. Twenty years is a long time and an even longer time when eight months of the year is spent on the road. And things had changed. They were older, the audience was younger, and the music at times seemed trumped by superficial details of the concerts.

The drug scene had always been there but now more than ever. Teenagers were going to Phish shows for drugs. And while tickets were never much of an issue for me or other seasoned fans, before any tour tickets sold on Ebay for three sometimes four times face value. And also the posters. For almost every show the band had an artist design a limited edition poster and, based solely on Internet sales, your poster, if you got in line early enough, doubled in value instantly.

But who really knows why Phish called it quits. Obviously it was Trey's decision and be his reasoning age or family or the degradation of the scene, he ended it all and that decision effected thousands of gypsies now done with touring or turning their attention to bands like Moe or String Cheese.

So of course this final concert, these last three sets had a weight to them unlike any concert I've ever been to. The air was thick with bittersweet emotion as thousands of hippies waited to see what songs Phish would play as a send off into the night and the resultant world, a world without the community of Phish.

With those first notes of Mike's Song, the audience snapped out of our somber stupor and danced feverishly. We danced like it was the last concert because we knew it was and that consciousness, that awareness created a reference in the crowd that manifested itself in individuals dancing wildly, joyously. Out of respect, we offered up our bodies in the way of dance. We were solipsistic only because we knew that's how the band wanted us.

Phish played like they played in the old days, the days during which I was a young teen with bootleg tapes as my only knowledge or experience of Phish.

And during set break, the crowd gasped for breath, regaining our composure. Only two more sets.

Tim, Charlie, Becca, and I rode the festival Ferris Wheel, and at its peak, looking out over the crowd of thousands, everything felt right. This was the only way to end it.

During Wading in the Velvet Sea, Page choked on the lyrics and tears dripped down his face. I'll admit, I grew teary and wrapped my arms around myself, careful not to look at anyone I knew. I wanted to share this moment with Page.

For those of you who haven't experienced Phish as I have, I know this must sound silly. During that song Page shared with us those sad emotions all of us had been feeling all weekend. And to know we were indeed sharing those feelings, not just amongst ourselves, but with the band, was an uncontrived and entirely necessary moment. Beautiful even.

And when Trey, Page, Mike, and Jon sang the acappella section of Glide, most everyone had tears in their eyes.

How often do you have the opportunity to say goodbye to a friend, someone with whom you've shared years of your life?

Even writing this now, I'm saying goodbye all over again.

When music speaks more than you ever thought it could, the experience is what I imagine a religious epiphany to be like. There

Set list 8/15/04

Set 1
    Mike's Song ->
    I am Hydrogen ->
    Weekapaug Groove
    Anything But Me
    Reba
    Carini ->
    Chalkdust Torture ->
    Possum
    Wolfman's Brother ->
    jam (the sexy bump) ->
    Wolfman's Brother ->
    Taste

Set 2
    Down With Disease ->
    Wading in the Velvet Sea
    Glide
    [band speech]
    Split Open and Melt ->
    jam (blowing off steam) ->
    Ghost

are powerful things in this world, things like invention and desire and fear and poetry and trust and music... things never to be underestimated.

That final Slave was unlike any song I've ever heard, and I've since refused to listen to the recording of it. Some moments cannot be captured or recorded and the moment Phish played that song at Coventry is one such moment.

During the song the audience made offerings of gratitude to the band. A dozen fans at first, then two dozen, then three and four, carried a gigantic egg-shaped white balloon from the farthest corner of the crowd all the way to the stage. Then, a long serpent of glowsticks made its way across the top of the audience to the stage, snaking and curling and dropping and lifting, almost every audience hand touched it.

The love and gratitude of the fans for this band was suddenly made tangible.

Phish has always been more than a band to me and most everyone else who has ever driven hundreds of miles to see a concert. And that final song, during which offerings were made and graciously accepted, the audience, these thousands of fans made and kept over two decades of musicianship, found a way to express their love and admiration for the music and the entire lifestyle support system that resulted.

Set 3
    Fast Enough for You
    Seven Below ->
    Simple ->
    Piper ->
    Bruno ->
    Dickie Scotland ->
    Wilson ->
    Slave to the Traffic Light
    [fireworks]

Encore
    [Trey speech]
    The Curtain

Then the band concluded with an encore and left the stage for the final time.

Walking back from the stage that night was a sobering event. Through the mud, knee-deep, surrounded by a thousand gypsy hippies, we made our way back to the runway and dispersed amidst the previously empty and undoubtedly ghostly campgrounds. Everyone was at that final concert and I can only imagine what the vast campsite may have felt like if you were the sole hippie wandering through it.

But now, after the show, we all made our way back home, or to vendors for food, or to pushers for drugs that would keep this evening from ending.

But it was already over.

And on that walk back I ran into all the friends I had sought out during the weekend. I saw Katie, Ryan, Oliver, Javier, Megan, Ethan, and George. But we had nothing to say to each other anymore. We merely smiled or in some cases hugged and kept on our separate paths. The concert was over. The trip was over. The connection we had, the music we shared, what originally brought us together and made us friends, was now a part of history.

The next morning I came out of my tent and found the campgrounds practically empty. Scores of caravans had already made their way to the runways and sat in line for their exit and what was surely a long drive home. Those still parked in the mud sat waiting for a truck to pull them out and those braver planned paths and had drivers floor the accelerator to hopefully gain enough momentum to plow through the muck to the road. That morning and into the afternoon was a day of quick getaways and muddy incarcerations.

The grounds were littered with trash and abandoned tents, shoes, gas grills, emergency now empty gas cans, and all other manner of a temporary civilization now abandoned. Even the Porta-Potties contained evidence of a now dead society and complete disregard for anyone coming to sift through the rubble.

And soon enough, the traffic started to move towards the exit and we followed, riding out of the festival grounds away from Coventry and south out of Vermont.

Tim and I had spent so much time together on tour that this last drive seemed to be a little too much and around Poughkeepsie we had one final difference of opinion and agreed that the best thing to do was to drop me off at the Poughkeepsie train station.

I then took the train into Manhattan's Grand Central Station where I hopped on the subway towards Brooklyn. I stood on the train simultaneously shocked and revitalized by the fluorescent lights and rocking motion and familiar stops of the subway.

Covered in mud, stinking from a week without showers, straddling my giant pack, I was that horrid pedestrian on the train. Commuters moved to opposite ends of the car, away from my stench. At some point, a homeless man, still dirtier and smellier than myself, made his way through the car asking riders for spare change and when he came to me he simply nodded and continued on his way.

Back in Brooklyn, I walked down Classon to my apartment and entered after only a brief struggle with my keys. Inside, the living room looked the same except a little more cluttered, a little dirtier than I left it. I set my pack on the floor and sat for a moment on the couch just resting, laughing at the fact that I woke up in Coventry in the mud earlier in the day. I needed a shower. I wanted to shit in a toilet that flushed.

I stepped into the bathroom and slapped on the light and stood bewildered by what I saw. The bathroom had been gutted. The bathtub was gone. The toilet gone. The sink gone. The wall tiling, the floor tiles, all of it gone. The bathroom was just an empty closet. I didn't even have it in me to laugh.

I just walked back into the living room and sat my muddy ass down on the couch.

The next day I called my roommate who more often than not sleept at his girlfriend's apartment and he said that the landlord had said they would be "renovating" the bathrooms. Soon after that discussion I noticed that a few items were missing from my bedroom including my video camera, my towels, and my piggy bank.

With only two weeks left in the apartment, only two weeks left in Bed-Stuy, they finally got me.

I tried to laugh it off, but really I just needed to get out of the house.

I went to a friendly, familiar, nearby coffee shop where I sat outside drinking a latte, smoking cigarettes, and reading *The New York Times*:

There are conflicting reports on whether Iraqi police or Shi'ite militiamen are in control of the Imam Ali Shrine in the city of Najaf. Sadr's Mahdi Army followers have been holed up in and around the Iman Ali mosque since fighting broke out anew in Najaf on August 5th. The standoff has been violent and deadly as the militiamen attack the encroaching Marines and then retreat through the cemetery to the Shrine.

THE LAST AMERICAN GYPSY

Najaf's Wadi Al Salam cemetery is one of the largest in the Muslim world. It is about 3.1 miles long and 1.86 miles wide.
August has is proving to be the deadliest month in the war thus far.

"Yo, dude!" someone said.//
I looked up and saw a hippie standing there in front of his muddy, crusty truck with Vermont license plates.
"Were you at Coventry?" he asked.
"Yeah," I said.
"Pretty bittersweet, huh?"

Made in the USA
San Bernardino, CA
14 April 2017